Fay
makes
it *easy*

Fay makes it easy

100 delicious recipes to impress with no stress

Fay Ripley

HarperCollins*Publishers*

Contents

'We must have a pie.
Stress cannot exist in the
presence of a pie.'
David Mamet

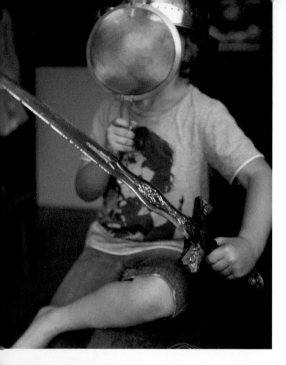

making it easy

In a world where food is political, powerful and controversial it's important to me to make the most of every morsel. My family and friends are the tick in my clock, and sharing time and great food with them is what makes the grotty bits of life palatable.

In this, my third book (I now have more books than kids), I have made sure there are 100 delicious recipes that will multi-task for you – that will strip away stress like a fake tan covers up cellulite. My No-knead Crusty Sunflower Loaf (see page 37) works for breakfast right through to a midnight snack; there's a super, tasty Salmon & Leek Lasagne (see page 96) with a cheaty sauce to save you time; while the Scandi Sharing Plate (see page 112) or Sushi Bites (see page 115) are great for a party, as a starter or a light lunch with the kids, and roasts like the Beef Ropa Vieja with Creamy Polenta (see page 75) will delight a tableful or can be used as leftovers during the week ahead. There's also a double serving of desserts that will make you look like a genius while leaving time for a cuppa and a box set.

Many of these work on a 'Stay at Home Tuesday' when time is tight and nerves are frayed, but are SO delicious and doable that you could easily serve them to a crowd. It's all about taking away the stress so that you can get back to loving the food you cook, the food you eat and the food you share.

Every meal has the potential to be a celebration, not only on a high day or holiday but also on a 'Washing Day Wednesday' or 'TGI Friday'. So I felt it was time to sort out the problem of 'What on earth am I going to cook?' when the boss/vicar/headmaster/boyfriend/girlfriend/old friend/ new friend/mother-in-law/neighbour/vet comes for breakfast, lunch or dinner.

It does seems that for a lot of us, the weekend is when family and friends get together, but it's only fun when you have the perfect recipe up your sleeve which will then leave you time to enjoy being king or queen of your castle.

This much I know; too many ingredients mean there is always something you can't find, don't have or simply forget to put in. Too much preparation means you don't get to brush your hair or teeth before it's time to eat. Techniques only used in restaurants that poach their eggs in nitric acid mean you lose confidence and your pride when it all goes wrong. And dear God, it does go wrong.

Not so long ago I found myself inviting a woman for dinner whom I admired tremendously. A grown-up girl crush and I wanted to impress the hell out of her. Bad start – I cared way too much about what she thought of me, my home and most of all my food. I started preparing weeks in advance. I gave the house an enema, terrified that my key guest might open a drawer and discover some skanky pant or other. I bleached the kids, shaved the dog and landscaped the garden. Then I began to plan the food; so I sent an email asking if she had any dietary requirements. Nothing. No response. I forged on with my banquet. A spring soup with peas, herbs and goat's cheese, homemade bread, an elaborate lamb dish that needed marinating for 40 days and 40 nights and a huge, I mean HUGE, pavlova. So huge was my pavlova I didn't even have a plate big enough to serve it on. So in my hosting madness, that was by now at tranquilliser stage, I made a plate … admittedly out of egg boxes and foil, but still. Things had clearly got out of hand. I was now swigging from any bottle I could get my hands on – cough mixture included – just to calm my perimenopausal hysteria. So, again I sent an email asking if there was anything she or her husband could or would not eat. No response until 20 minutes before they pulled up outside my house when I received a text saying, 'Hi, forgot to mention that we are both off dairy, meat, wheat, sugar and alcohol. Soz, hope that's ok, don't go to any trouble! :)'

OOOOOOOOOMMMMMMMMGGGGGGGGGG. Don't go to any trouble? I was more relaxed when I had my coil fitted. As I looked up from my phone in despair, the fire

alarm sounded and screams of 'The bread! The bread! It's on fire!' came from my now smoke-filled kitchen/diner. Some early, helpful guests threw their cardigans on the smouldering remains and assured me that crackers would be just as good.

Well, I now had 15 minutes to produce a meal for the guests of honour using only a tin of mung beans and some coconut water. Quickly I knocked up what I could, given the brief. Although I admit I did pass off the soup as vegetable-based when it actually had a chicken stock at its very core and was laced with dairy products (she was no vegetarian, just on a blinking diet, so I figured it was only a white lie). So I fussed and fettled all through a hideous night of stress-soaked dishes I wished I had never tried to reproduce in a domestic environment.

Then came the pavlova – in all its glory and on its tailor-made cardboard plate. Drum roll please. But do you know? She didn't even glance up. She just flicked her hand into my face as though stopping traffic and said 'Not for me'. 'The hand.' I was just about to tip the most glorious pudding I had ever made right on top of her blow-dried head when from my son's baby monitor I heard the unmistakable sound of retching followed by a scream that only dogs and mums can hear.

I spent the rest of the night with buckets and sponges knowing that I had impressed no one, least of all myself. Oh, and by the way, she never even texted a thank you. Nothing. I haven't seen her since. I no longer have a girl crush on her and I fully intend to give her more than just 'the hand' when I do bump into her.

However, it was in the cold light of day that I pledged to follow some simple rules from then on. Rules to make life easier, to make life fun and rules that would mean you and I could enjoy sharing our food without beads of sweat dripping into the gravy. I now stack my pavlova in layers to great effect (see page 223) so there's no need to customise the crockery, and although I do swig from the odd bottle every now and then, it's usually not because dinner's gone tits up.

So, the boxes that every recipe in this book must tick are:

☑ Not too many ingredients.

☑ You don't have to source the ingredients from the foothills of the Himalayas.

☑ You don't have to faff about with fiddly bits.

☑ There must be a mouthwatering picture of the finished product for each and every recipe so you can see what the hell you are heading towards.

☑ Simple instructions that work every time.

☑ It has to look like it's taken you ages to prepare even though it didn't.

☑ Show-off value must be high.

☑ It must be absolutely, totally delicious.

☑ It's got to be as good for you to cook as them to eat.

☑ It must be stress free.

☑ (Oh, and never invite guests with no manners and/or who will only eat dishes made from water and lemon balm.)

My food always comes from my kitchen and my heart. I hope these recipes will solve a few problems and put smiles on faces, yours included. This is the food I eat and this is the food I love to share. It's about de-stressing, delicious grub and being able to enjoy sitting round a table with folk you want make memories with.

I'm working on making the rest of life easy … you might have to bear with me on that one.

Fay x

by the way...

In all recipes I try to use:

☑ Free-range eggs & chicken

☑ British beef & pork

☑ Sustainable fish

'When you wake up in the morning, Pooh,' said Piglet at last, 'what's the first thing you say to yourself?'

'What's for breakfast?' said Pooh. 'What do you say, Piglet?'

'I say, I wonder what's going to happen exciting today?' said Piglet.

Pooh nodded thoughtfully. 'It's the same thing,' he said.

A. A. Milne

morning glory

morning glory

Seedy Breakfast Bars

Breakfasts, lunch boxes, snacks or with ice cream, these feel good enough to eat without too much guilt. If, like me, you are comfortable with a little guilt, melt dark chocolate and, once the bars have cooled, drizzle it all over them. Lick the bowl and pray for forgiveness.

For 16
Prep time... 15 mins
Cook time... 35 mins
(plus cooling and setting)

All you need is...

150g butter, cubed
80g (4 tbsp) golden syrup
100g (2 heaped tbsp) apricot jam
250g oats
200g currants
100g pumpkin seeds
50g sesame seeds
50g sunflower seeds

All you do is...

1 Preheat the oven to 160°C (fan), 180°C, gas mark 4. Line a brownie tin or baking tray, around 20 x 30cm, with baking paper.

2 In a large pan, gently melt the butter, golden syrup and jam, then stir in all the other ingredients to evenly coat.

3 Scrape the lot into your lined tin and with the back of a large spoon firmly smooth the mixture down as flat as you can, moulding the mixture right to the edges of the tin.

4 Bake for 30 minutes till golden on top. Cool at room temperature for 30 minutes then pop in the fridge to set for at least 1 hour before cutting into 16 bars.

✓ De-stress
These keep brilliantly in an airtight container in the fridge for 3–4 days.

Special Birthday Breakfast Swiss Roll

Most of the time we rush through breakfast as we rush through life. Well, every now and then let's celebrate the fact that it's the beginning of the day and who knows what fabulousness lies ahead. This is a fruit-filled, yogurt-covered fluffy pancake with celebration at its heart, where every day is somebody's birthday.

For 4–6
Prep time... 15 mins
Cook time... 10 mins (plus cooling)
❄ (cake only)

All you need is...

3 large eggs
75g unrefined golden caster sugar
75g self-raising flour, sifted
2 tbsp raspberry jam
1 large banana, peeled and sliced
170g pot Greek yogurt
a sprinkling of dark brown sugar
225g raspberries, washed

All you do is...

1 Preheat the oven to 200°C (fan), 220°C, gas mark 7. Line the base and sides of a brownie or Swiss roll tin, 20 x 30cm, with baking paper.

2 In a large bowl with an electric hand whisk, whizz the eggs and sugar for 4–5 minutes till pale, frothy and like thick double cream.

3 Fold in the flour to completely combine then scrape into your brownie tin and bake for 10 minutes till lightly golden and springy.

4 Put a large piece of baking paper on the worktop and flip the sponge onto it as soon as it comes out of the oven. Peel off the baking paper from the top of the sponge and while still hot, roll up within the new piece of baking paper. Leave it to cool (this will help the sponge hold its shape and not crack later).

5 When cool and ready to serve, unroll the sponge, discard the paper and spread the jam evenly all over the sponge, not quite to the edge. Place the banana slices down the near side and gently roll the sponge over.

To serve

Just dollop the Greek yogurt along the top of the roll, sprinkle with the dark brown sugar and scatter on the raspberries. Slice and serve immediately.

Wholemeal French Toast with Maple Syrup & Blueberries

Using brown bread gives this romantic breakfast classic a nutty hearty flavour that sings a love song to those berries. Perfect for a celebration or a Sunday special, the bacon is optional – but not if you are me.

For 2
Prep time... 5 mins
Cook time... 15 mins

All you need is...

2 large eggs
100ml milk
1 tsp ground cinnamon
4 rashers smoked streaky bacon
    (optional)
2 knobs of butter
4 thick slices of wholemeal/brown
    bread
a couple of handfuls of blueberries
maple syrup, for drizzling

All you do is...

1 In a large bowl, whisk together the eggs, milk and cinnamon.

2 If having the bacon, fry it up in a non-stick frying pan till crispy. Set aside in a warming oven.

3 Melt a knob of butter in a large non-stick frying pan over a medium heat. Dip the bread in your egg mix for a few seconds on each side to allow it to soak up some of the mix and fry 2 slices at a time, for 1–2 minutes on each side, till golden. Transfer to your warming oven while the next batch cooks.

4 Assemble by slicing the French toast into large triangles.

To serve
If you've given in to the dark side, arrange the bacon on top, then scatter over the berries and finish with a drizzle of maple syrup.

Brekky Hangover Sub

For 2
Prep time... 10 mins
Cook time... 15 mins

Dan, my Aussie husband, was apparently brought up on Subs – that's a baguette loaded with goodies to you and me. This one is his favourite hangover cure or post-surfer's brunch. They do breakfast very well Down Under.

All you need is...

6 streaky smoked bacon rashers
1 small baguette (about 200–250g)
4 squirts tomato purée (4 tsp)
2 tsp Dijon mustard
2 medium tomatoes, sliced
1 ripe avocado, halved and sliced
80g Cheddar, grated

All you do is...

1 Preheat the grill to medium-high and line the grill tray with foil. Fry the bacon in a large non-stick frying pan till crispy on both sides.

2 Cut the baguette in half lengthways and lightly grill on both sides.

3 Spread 2 squirts of tomato purée over the cut base of each baguette half, followed by 1 teaspoon of mustard on each. Tear over the bacon, then alternate the tomatoes and avocado across the top. Pile on the grated Cheddar and put the baguette halves back on the lined tray under the grill for just a minute or two to melt the cheese till it starts to bubble.

To serve
Cut each sub in half.

✓ Impress
Serve with garlic mayo on the side.

Idiot-proof Peanut Butter

For 2 jars (600g)
Prep time... 10 mins
Cook time... 12 mins

When our lovely friend Gemma pops over I demand she brings a jar of her delicious homemade peanut butter, which she insists is soooo easy any idiot could make it. Well, this idiot tried and failed, it just wasn't as good as hers. So I made her come over and make it with me … To stop anyone calling you an idiot, here's the oh-so-simple recipe from her to me, tried and tested, and me to you … It's crunchy, moreish, full of goodness and just wonderful on a thick slice of toast.

All you need is...

600g peanuts, skins on (or blanched
    if you can't find them)
1 tbsp runny honey
½ tsp sea salt
1 tbsp groundnut or peanut oil

All you do is...

1 Preheat the oven to 160°C (fan), 180°C, gas mark 4. Spread the peanuts out on a roasting tray and roast for about 12–15 minutes to just golden, but watch them. Cool.

2 When the nuts have cooled, put them in a food processor and pulse a couple of times. Remove 2 tablespoons of the nuts and set aside. Now blitz the remaining nuts for 2–3 minutes, stir, then blitz again for another 2–3 minutes until smooth and oily (it's the blitzing that brings out the oil). Add the honey, salt and groundnut or peanut oil and whizz to combine. Finally, stir in the reserved chopped nuts.

3 Scrape the peanut butter into sterilised jars.

✓ De-stress
Sterilise the jars in the dishwasher.
✓ Impress
Make a loaf (p37) to go with it!

Wild Mushrooms on Toast

For 1
Prep time... 5 mins
Cook time... 5 mins

By all means, feel free to get up early and forage barefoot in the forest for some wild local mushrooms or … just buy a pack from your nearest supermarket. The combo of mushrooms, cream and thyme oozes luxury but takes just minutes to cook. It's a weekend breakfast, a busy brunch or even a Friday tea – you pick the time, even if you can't pick the mushrooms.

All you need is...

a knob of butter
2 sprigs thyme, leaves only
100g wild mushrooms, torn if large
1 tbsp single cream
½ tsp Dijon mustard
2 slices sourdough, toasted
30g mature Cheddar, grated

All you do is...

1 Preheat the grill to a medium-high setting.

2 Heat a non-stick frying pan, add the butter and when it's foaming throw in the thyme leaves and mushrooms to fry for 3 minutes till soft. Add the cream and mustard. Mix well with some seasoning.

3 Divide the creamy mushrooms and pile onto the toasts, then cover with the cheese. Pop under the grill for just a couple of minutes until the cheese starts to brown and bubble.

✓ De-stress
If you can't find wild mushrooms, just use portobello mushrooms, thinly sliced.

✓ Impress
Drizzle with some truffle oil for an extra-special treat.

Morning Muffins

'Come and see my muffins, darling! They're warm and you don't often get the chance!' This is what my husband wakes up to ... I know how to keep my marriage alive.

For 6 muffins
Prep time... 10 mins
Cook time... 25 mins

All you need is...

120g unsalted butter
250g self-raising wholemeal flour
50g soft brown sugar, plus a little
    extra for the top
zest of 2 lemons
125ml milk
1 large egg
6 heaped tsp raspberry jam
6 fresh raspberries, to decorate
    (optional)

All you do is...

1 Preheat the oven to 180°C (fan), 200°C, gas mark 6. Line a 6-hole muffin tray with paper muffin cases.

2 Gently melt the butter in a small pan and set aside. In a large bowl, mix the flour and sugar. Add the lemon zest and combine well.

3 Whisk the milk, melted butter and egg in a jug and pour into the dry ingredients. Fold together.

4 Plop 1 dessertspoon of the mix into the bottom of each paper case. Make a small dent and add a heaped teaspoon of jam to the middle of each. Now divide the rest of the mixture equally, covering the jam. Sprinkle with a little extra sugar and, if using, pop a raspberry on top. Bake for 25 minutes. Cool in the tin for 10 minutes, so the jam doesn't scald, before serving.

To serve

Eat warm with butter for sheer perfection. Best on the day they're made but happy to be re-warmed a few hours after making.

✓ De-stress

Get the tin and cases ready and mix the dry ingredients in a bowl the night before ... then it's a 5-minute job in the morning to throw these together.

Lemon Ricotta Hotcakes

For 4–6
Prep time... 10 mins
Cook time... 15 mins

Dan was born and bred on the shores of Sydney, Australia. He mainly misses obvious stuff like sun, sea and surf, but he also goes gooey-eyed at the mention of ricotta hotcakes, a Sydney breakfast staple he lived off from the brilliant Bill Granger's café. So when he's feeling homesick, I turn the kitchen lights on full blast, splash him with washing-up water and fry up these delicious, soft pillows of golden mouthfuls to complete his trip 'down under' memory lane. It's a lot cheaper than the airfare.

All you need is...

250g ricotta
150ml milk
2 large eggs, separated
zest of 1 lemon, plus 1 to serve
100g plain flour
1 tsp baking powder
30g butter
caster sugar, to serve

All you do is...

1 In a large bowl, mix the ricotta, milk, egg yolks and lemon zest with a fork or whisk till smooth. Fold in the flour and baking powder to combine.

2 In a separate large clean bowl, whisk the egg whites to soft peaks then gently fold into the ricotta mix.

3 Heat a good knob of butter in a large non-stick frying pan and ladle a tablespoon of the batter into the sizzling butter. Fry for 1–2 minutes on each side until firm and golden.

To serve
Cut both lemons into large wedges. Squeeze lemon juice over the warm pancakes and sprinkle with caster sugar.

✓ Impress
Drizzle over some strawberry jam.

No-knead Crusty Sunflower Loaf with Cream Cheese & Blackberries

For 6, makes a 1kg loaf
Prep time... 5 mins
Cook time... 45 mins (plus cooling)

This is a quick miracle loaf – a miracle because it's a no-knead, no-waiting bread that is crunchy on the outside and soft inside. If you've never made bread before this is a great place to start. You can pair it with breakfast goodies, salads, lunches and teas alike; soft butter and jam is my old-school favourite, but do try the cream cheese and blackberries for a proper farmhouse feel …

All you need is...

a little olive oil
500g plain wholemeal or spelt flour
2 x 7g sachets fast-acting dried yeast
1 tsp salt
150g sunflower seeds
500ml warm water

To serve
200g soft cream cheese
250g blackberries
squeezy runny honey, for drizzling

All you do is...

1 Preheat the oven to 180°C (fan), 200°C, gas mark 6. Oil a 1kg/2lb loaf tin with a little olive oil.

2 In a large bowl, mix all the dry bread ingredients together, holding back a handful of sunflower seeds. Pour in the warm water and gently bring together with a wooden spoon into a wet dough.

3 Scrape into the tin, sprinkle over the extra seeds and bake for 45 minutes. Remove from the tin and cool for 30 minutes. Cut into thick slices.

To serve
Eat warm with a thick spread of cream cheese, a handful of blackberries and a drizzle of runny honey.

✓ De-stress
Best eaten straightaway but it also toasts up a treat.
✓ Impress
It will.

Fry-up Breakfast Pizza

For 4
Prep time... 5 mins
Cook time... 10 mins

I sort of discovered this by mistake when frying some eggs at a friend's house. I suddenly realised they only had one pan, so I threw the rest of my ingredients on top in a last-minute panic. It was a big hit and has now become a breakfast, lunch and quick dinner regular, with those Italian flavours making it all look like a clever plan not a silly mistake. Phew!

All you need is...

2 tbsp olive oil
100g chestnut mushrooms, sliced
6 large eggs
6 cherry tomatoes, halved
2-3 slices smoked ham
a few fresh basil leaves
2 tbsp finely grated Parmesan cheese
ciabatta bread, to serve, warmed

All you do is...

1 Heat 1 tablespoon olive oil in a large non-stick frying pan and fry the mushrooms for 3–4 minutes till soft. Take them out and set aside.

2 Crack each egg into separate cups or ramekins so you can quickly get them into the pan without breaking the yolks. Now heat another tablespoon of olive oil in the same frying pan. Gently slip each egg into the pan around the edges then one in the middle, so all the egg whites join up.

3 Straightaway, pop on the cherry tomato halves (cut side up), avoiding the yolks, then scatter the cooked mushrooms. Tear over the ham and basil leaves and sprinkle the Parmesan over the whole lot. Cook for another minute until the egg whites have set and the cheese is beginning to melt. Season and serve.

To serve
Take the pan to your table and cut pizza-shaped triangles with a yolk per person. Serve with warm ciabatta bread.

✓ Impress
Add a drizzle of chilli oil or chilli sauce for those that like a kick.

Fay's Florentine Me Muffins

For 1
Prep time... 5 mins
Cook time... 5 mins

I make this for me. Just for me, as a treat because I don't get handbags and massages any more. It's a classic combo of garlic, spinach, soft egg and salty Parmesan on a deep doughy base. Easy to knock up for a weekend breakfast, brunch or light lunch and you can just multiply the ingredients if 'me time' is sparse and there's more of a crowd.

All you need is...

1 tbsp olive oil
1 garlic clove, peeled and crushed
100g baby spinach leaves
1 English muffin, halved
2 medium eggs
2 tbsp finely grated Parmesan
25g black pitted Greek olives
    (Kalamata), chopped

All you do is...

1 In a medium pan, heat the olive oil then fry the crushed garlic for a minute till just golden. Add the spinach leaves and stir for a minute more to soften.

2 Meanwhile, lightly toast the muffin halves and top them with the spinach. Then fry the eggs in a non-stick frying pan till just cooked but with a runny yolk, about 3 minutes.

3 Sprinkle some Parmesan onto each egg and scatter over the chopped olives to finish.

My Hollywood Raspberry Bircher Muesli

For 6–8
Prep time... 5 mins
(plus overnight soaking)
Cook time... None

I was once a granola-only girl, stubbornly shunning this smooth, creamy, breakfast muesli because I thought it was only for Hollywood types with henna tattoos. But once bitten, forever smitten. You only need a small bowlful, as it's packed with goodness and sets the whole family up for a hectic day. The Ripleys are now properly addicted to this LA morning energy booster.

All you need is...

200g rolled oats
200ml apple juice
80ml milk
2 apples
125g fresh raspberries
200g raspberry yogurt
25g roasted hazelnuts, chopped

All you do is...

1 Mix the oats, apple juice and milk together then coarsely grate in the apples (skin on) and mix well.

2 Add the raspberries and yogurt and stir together. Leave covered in the fridge overnight. Add a drop of milk in the morning if needed.

To serve
Scatter the roasted hazelnuts on top.

✓ De-stress
Keeps really well covered in the fridge for up to 3 days.
✓ Impress
Add a sprinkling of granola (homemade or bought) and some extra berries.

"'Tis an ill cook that cannot lick his own fingers.'

William Shakespeare

Wasabi sesame tuna with crispy
noodle salad

Speedy horseradish soda bread

Baked tahini salmon

Sweetcorn & mint fritters with
griddled halloumi

Sweet magic kale

Italian holiday schnitzel with aglio e olio

Mexican chicken soup with salsa
& corn chips

Creamy salmon & leek lasagne

let's do
lunch

Grandma's Perfect Pastry

Makes 400g
Prep time... 10 mins
Cook time... 20 mins
❄

My grandmother, Ivy, helped bring me up. Her main grandparenting tool was her pastry; so light and perfect it made the naughtiest of children putty in her hands as we all begged for a minced pie or jam tart. She said you have to have pastry hands to get the crumb right. Sadly she went to her grave taking the recipe and her pastry hands with her. Here's my version that I hope comes with Ivy's blessing.

All you need is...

250g plain flour
140g butter, chilled and cubed
a pinch of salt
2 tbsp iced water

All you do is...

1 In a food processor, whizz the flour, butter and salt to fine crumbs then pour in the water to bring it together into a ball.

2 Gather up the dough and roll it out between 2 sheets of baking paper to fit the tin you're using – aim for about 5mm thickness – and trim the edges.

3 Use the pastry trimmings to patch up any holes then prick the base a few times with a fork and chill in the fridge for 30 minutes.

4 Preheat the oven to 200°C (fan), 220°C, gas mark 7. Blind-bake the pastry case (with baking beans or rice on top of baking paper) for 15 minutes. Remove the paper and beans then bake for another 5 minutes. Set aside till ready to fill.

✓ De-stress
Use your fingers to rub the flour and butter together if you don't have a food processor.

✓ Impress
Experiment by adding chopped herbs, mustard powder, spices or grated citrus zest to flavour the pastry depending on what recipe you're using it for.

Griddled Salad with Soft Egg & Bacon

Grilling the lettuce hearts lifts this salad to great heights. Barbecue them and it literally flies away. It can be a lunch, brunch or starter salad. My kids love the sweet tangy dressing so it's become a favourite after-school supper for my lot that's ready in minutes.

For 4
Prep time... 10 mins
Cook time... 10 mins

All you need is...

4 large eggs
8-12 slices pancetta or streaky
    smoked bacon
4 baby gem lettuce hearts
1 tbsp extra virgin olive oil
fresh sourdough or soda bread,
    sliced, to serve

Dressing
2 tsp Dijon mustard
1 tsp runny honey
1 tbsp white wine vinegar
4 tbsp extra virgin olive oil

All you do is...

1 Pop the eggs on to boil (see instructions below). When they're ready, slice each in half.

2 Preheat a griddle pan or non-stick frying pan and cook the pancetta or bacon till crispy. Set aside.

3 Cut the lettuce heads in half from top to bottom then brush the cut sides with the olive oil. In the same pan pop the lettuces, cut side down, to griddle and begin to char (it's those lines you are after). It will take 2–3 minutes; turn to briefly cook the other side.

4 Make the dressing in a small jug by whisking the mustard, honey, vinegar and olive oil with seasoning till creamy.

5 Now griddle or toast some thick slices of your favourite bread.

To serve
Place the lettuce on top of the toast, then a couple of slices of pancetta or bacon and 2 halves of an egg. Drizzle with plenty of your sweet dressing.

✓ Perfect softly-boiled eggs every time
Put your eggs (at room temperature) into cold water and bring to the boil. Time 4 minutes from the start of boiling and keep them at a gentle simmer. Take them all out and gently break all the shells to stop them cooking further. Then remove the shells under cold running water so you can handle them.

Italian Sausage Roll Pasta Bake

This rich, super savoury alternative to lasagne is beyond moreish. Authentically Italian in flavour, it's tasty enough to serve to a visiting crowd or make just for your homies.

For 6
Prep time... 15 mins
Cook time...1 hour
❄

All you need is...

2 tbsp olive oil
1 large onion, peeled and
    finely chopped
250g Portabello mushrooms,
    finely chopped
30g bunch fresh sage, leaves finely
    chopped (keep back a handful)
450g good-quality sausagemeat
200g tomato purée
150ml dry white wine
250g pack fresh lasagne sheets
600ml tomato passata
200ml half-fat crème fraîche

All you do is...

1 Preheat the oven to 160°C (fan), 180°C, gas mark 4.

2 In a non-stick frying pan, heat a splash of olive oil and cook the onion for 10 minutes to soften. Throw in the chopped mushrooms and fry for another 5 minutes, then add the sage and cook for another minute.

3 Now put the sausagemeat in. Using a wooden spoon, break it up into a mince as it browns. Keep turning it over for a few minutes to cook it right through then add the tomato purée, stirring for another minute or two. Add the wine and let it bubble for 5 minutes. Season.

3 Using scissors, cut each lasagne sheet in half to make rectangles. Lay them all out and divide the filling evenly between the sheets. Roll each pasta sheet around the filling to make short stubby cannelloni rolls and arrange them in a 22 x 26cm shallow ovenproof dish in a single layer.

4 Mix the passata and crème fraîche together in a large jug with some seasoning and pour over the pasta. Toss the last few sage leaves in olive oil and scatter over the top.

5 Pop in the oven for 40 minutes.

✓ De-stress

I often put this together the day before, keep it in the fridge then cook it in the oven (it will need 10–15 minutes longer if cooked straight from the fridge).

Taramasalata with Baby Tomato Salad

Homemade taramasalata tastes nothing like the bright pink version in the shops and is always a talking point as a result. Perfect as a starter or light lunch. You don't need much of this rich smoky pâté, just spread it thinly on warm bread dipped in the fresh tomato juices and it will make the Greek sun shine on you even on a rainy day.

For 4–6 (makes 300g)
Prep time... 10 mins
Cook time... None

All you need is...

40g soft white bread, no crusts
10g bunch fresh chives
160g smoked cod's roe
juice of 1 lemon
8 tbsp olive oil
warm crusty bread,
    to serve

All you do is...

1 Put the bread and chives in a food processor and whizz to very fine breadcrumbs. Peel off and discard the skin of the cod's roe, adding the roe, lemon juice and olive oil to the processor.

2 Whizz till smooth. Serve spread on slices of warm crusty bread.

Baby Tomato Salad

All you need is...

500g cherry or baby tomatoes, washed
2 tbsp olive oil
2 tsp red wine vinegar
30g bunch fresh basil

All you do is...

1 Halve the tomatoes and pop in a serving bowl, drizzle over the olive oil and the vinegar with some seasoning. Tear in the basil leaves and toss.

✓ Impress
Use a mix of red, yellow and green tomatoes – when you can find them.

Parma Ham
& Melon Risotto

For 4
Prep time... 10 mins
Cook time... 25 mins

25 years ago, in a flat in Shepherds Bush, my lovely pal Matthew, who I haven't really seen since, made an amazing risotto for a bunch of us struggling actors. The memory of this tasty dish has sadly stayed with me longer than our friendship, as the combination of salty ham and sweet melon flesh is inspired. He's a big-shot producer now; perhaps I should give him a call and invite him over for some risotto and a catch up.

All you need is...

1 large onion, peeled and finely chopped
1 tbsp olive oil
20g butter
250g risotto rice
100ml rosé or white wine
900ml chicken stock
60g Pecorino or Parmesan, finely grated
80g Parma ham slices, roughly chopped
1 small sweet melon, e.g. Galia, deseeded and flesh roughly diced

All you do is...

1 In a large non-stick frying pan, fry the onion in the oil and butter till soft, about 5 minutes.

2 Add the rice and stir for a minute or so, then add the wine and bubble off the alcohol for 2–3 minutes. Pour in the stock, bring to the boil, stir once, then turn the heat down. Pop a lid on and simmer for 15 minutes till the rice is cooked but still has a little bite.

3 Now stir through most of the cheese, the Parma ham and season with lots of pepper. Leave covered for 5 minutes to rest.

To serve

Just before serving, scatter over the diced melon and the remaining cheese.

✓ De-stress
This makes a brilliant first course, the above amount is perfect for 6 people.

✓ Impress
Use a melon-ball scoop for proper 70s show-off balls.

Roasted Tomato & Pepper Soup with Sweet Basil Yogurt

My kids are fussy with soup but cheer up on a Tuesday for this after-school classic. It has appeal over all seasons as it feels warm and wintery served in mugs on a foggy autumn day and yet full of midsummer Mediterranean promise with a glass of Rioja and some grown-ups. Try it cold with crushed ice and a splash of vodka, although maybe not on a cheer-up Tuesday with the kids.

For 4–6 (makes 1.5 litres)
Prep time... 10 mins
Cook time... 35 mins
❄ (soup only)

All you need is...

1kg ripe tomatoes, halved
2 red peppers, halved and deseeded
1 red onion, peeled and quartered
3 garlic cloves, whole in their skin
2 tbsp olive oil
500ml vegetable or chicken stock
100g Greek yogurt
15g fresh basil, finely chopped
a squirt of runny honey

All you do is...

1 Preheat the oven to 180°C (fan), 200°C, gas mark 6. Chuck the tomatoes, peppers, onion and garlic cloves into a large oven tray. Season, drizzle with the oil and roast for 35–40 minutes till soft and starting to char a little.

2 Squeeze the soft garlic flesh from the cloves (discard the skin) into a large pan and scrape in all the roasted veg. Pour in the stock and whizz with a hand blender till fairly smooth but with a little texture. Heat gently until just bubbling.

To serve

Mix the yogurt and basil with a squirt of honey and slip a dessertspoon onto the top of each bowl of warm soup.

✓ De-stress
Make a day or two before, as it gets better when left overnight, covered, in the fridge.
✓ Impress
Serve with No-knead Crusty Sunflower Loaf (see p37).

Brie Baked Bubble & Squeak

For 4
Prep time... 15 mins
Cook time... 40 mins

I love a hearty vegetarian dish that really delivers and this soft tasty bake will comfort you with creamy cheese, the crunch of cabbage and the kick of a little chilli ... Obviously throw in a bit of chorizo when frying the onions if you feel the need to 'pork it up', but for those avoiding livestock it's an easy simple lunch or supper dish to share.

All you need is...

800g potatoes
240g bag ready-shredded cabbage and leek
2 tbsp olive oil
2 garlic cloves, peeled and crushed
1 red chilli, deseeded and finely chopped (optional, but really good)
200g cherry tomatoes, halved
200g brie or dolcelatte, roughly chopped
3 large eggs, beaten
green salad leaves, to serve

All you do is...

1 Preheat the oven to 160°C (fan), 180°C, gas mark 4.

2 Wash and chop the potatoes into small bite-sized chunks, leaving the skin on. Par-boil in salted water for 8–10 minutes, then drain.

3 Meanwhile, in a frying pan, cook the cabbage and leek mix in 1 tablespoon olive oil for 2–3 minutes then add the garlic and cook for another minute. Season.

4 Toss in the chilli (if using), tomatoes, brie or dolcelatte and eggs with 1 more tablespoon of the olive oil. Give the whole thing a good stir and transfer to a large, shallow, ovenproof ceramic dish and bake for 30 minutes till bubbling and crispy on top.

To serve
Serve in your oven dish on a big wooden board with a bowlful of green leaves and some warm crusty bread.

✓ De-stress
Shred the cabbage and leek yourself if you can't find a prepared bag.

Lentil-stuffed Peppers with Falafel Topping

Team this with lamb or fish or serve as a centrestage veggie option. The falafel crumbs go crispy and the salty feta pings through all those Mediterranean flavours. All it really needs is a green salad and some crusty bread.

For 4
Prep time... 15 mins
Cook time... 35 mins

All you need is...

4 large red peppers
400g tin green lentils, drained and rinsed
12 sun-dried tomatoes in oil, drained and finely chopped
30g fresh basil, leaves chopped
150g feta
1 tbsp balsamic vinegar
4 tbsp olive oil
8 ready-made falafel balls (chilled aisle of supermarket)
½ red chilli, deseeded

All you do is...

1 Preheat the oven to 180°C (fan), 200°C, gas mark 6.

2 Halve and deseed the peppers, trying to keep the halves and stalks intact (cut through the stalks). Put them cut side up in a large ovenproof dish.

3 Mix the lentils with the chopped sun-dried tomatoes and basil. Crumble in the feta and dress with the vinegar and olive oil. Season. Fill the pepper halves with the lentil mix. Make the topping by blitzing the falafel balls and chilli in a food processor until they look like breadcrumbs, then spoon generously over the filled peppers.

4 Bake for 35 minutes, covering halfway through with foil if the breadcrumbs are getting too dark.

✓ Impress
Finish with a drizzle of basil oil; simply whizz a pack of basil leaves with a few generous tablespoons of olive oil and season; drizzle over the peppers just before serving.

Nutty Green Roast Veg Gratin

A veggie showstopper that's good enough to be a headline dish without needing too much attention from you. It's perfect with all manner of roasts and I love it with A Greek Barbie (see p199).

For 6 (side) or 4 (main)
Prep time... 15 mins
Cook time... 50 mins

All you need is...

2 leeks, trimmed and chopped
3 courgettes, sliced
2 green peppers, deseeded and sliced
2 tbsp olive oil
130g pot fresh green pesto
　　(or make your own, see p143)

For the topping
25g Parmesan, finely grated
50g shelled pistachios
1 thick slice of wholemeal or white
　　bread (50g), leave crusts on
1 tbsp olive oil

All you do is...

1 Preheat the oven to 200°C (fan), 220°C, gas mark 7.

2 In a big bowl, toss the leeks, courgettes and peppers in the oil and pesto with some seasoning.

3 Spread the vegetables out in a large ovenproof dish and bake for 20 minutes. Stir and bake for a further 20 minutes.

4 Make the topping by blitzing the Parmesan, pistachios, oil and the bread in a food processer to a rough crumb.

5 Top the vegetables with the nutty crumbs and bake for another 10 minutes until golden and crisp.

✓ De-stress
Get all the vegetables ready the day or morning before and pre-blitz your topping.

Poached Chinese Chook (to go with Mash & Peas)

Like Fred and Ginger, Burton and Taylor or Ian and Janette Krankie, chicken and mash are the perfect bedfellows. It's a combo that calms me in a crisis; with the sweet, sharp, minty dressing it's one of my favourite Sunday lunch specials. Easily good enough to serve a crowd or keep all for yourself … comfort on a plate.

For 4–5
Prep time… 15 mins
Cook time… 1 hour 30 mins
❄

All you need is...

1.5kg whole chicken
1 large onion, peeled and roughly sliced
a knob of fresh ginger, peeled and sliced
4 garlic cloves, skin left on and smashed
2 celery sticks, halved
150ml glass dry sherry, e.g. Amontillado (optional)

Dressing
5cm piece of fresh ginger, peeled and finely grated
2 tbsp light soy sauce
1 tbsp toasted sesame oil
30g pack fresh mint, leaves chopped
30g pack fresh basil, leaves chopped
juice of 1 lime
1 red chilli, deseeded and finely chopped

All you do is...

1 Pop the whole chicken on top of the slices of onion in a large pot (8-litre capacity), adding the ginger, garlic, celery and sherry along with 2–3 litres cold water to cover. Slowly bring to the boil, put a lid on and simmer for 1 hour. Remove the pan from the heat and leave to rest in the pot for another 30 minutes.

2 For the dressing, whisk together the ginger, soy sauce, sesame oil, mint, basil, lime juice and chilli in a small bowl and add 100ml of the cooking liquor.

3 Now remove the chicken, let it rest for 10 minutes on a tray or board, then shred all the meat, discarding the skin.

To serve
Serve the chicken on a big platter on top of smooth mashed potatoes with the dressing poured over and a side of soya beans or petits pois.

✓ Impress
For heaven-sent mash, get your hands on a potato ricer – I resisted for years but I am now a convert.
✓ Other stuff
Use that stock or freeze it … it's gold.

My Seaside Quick Roast

For 4
Prep time... 10 mins
Cook time... 15 mins

The combo of fish is up to you, as long as you keep the pieces all fairly similar in size. Like some kind of holy miracle it is literally thrown into a piping hot oven and comes out as an unforgettable feast. Simple flavours with juice you will want to soak up with crusty bread. Serve with a glass of white wine, a sunset and a bible.

All you need is...

1 whole squid, cleaned, cartilage removed
2–4 small pin-boned sea bass fillets, or bigger ones halved
4 scallops, muscle trimmed off, leave roe on
4–8 large king prawns in shell
1 or 2 skate wings, halved
1 lemon, plus 1 cut into wedges, to serve
2 garlic cloves, peeled and crushed
1 fresh red chilli, deseeded and finely chopped
100g samphire, rinsed well
100ml (½ large glass) dry white wine
2 tbsp extra virgin olive oil

All you do is...

1 Preheat the oven to its highest setting, approximately 220°C (fan), 240°C, gas mark 9. Slice the squid into thick rings.

2 Spread out all the fish and shellfish in a large shallow baking tray. Finely zest the lemon over the fish then halve it and throw the pieces into the tray.

3 Season then scatter over the crushed garlic, finely chopped chilli and the samphire. Pour over the wine and drizzle in the olive oil, turning the ingredients with your hands gently to coat.

4 Put the tray in the oven for about 15 minutes, until everything is cooked through. Remove the tray and then, using a pair of tongs, carefully squeeze the hot lemon all over the top.

To serve
Serve with extra lemon wedges, a big green salad and crusty bread for dunking. Also great with Sweet Magic Kale (see p91).

✓ De-stress
Ask the fishmonger or person behind the fish counter to do as much of the trimming, cleaning and cutting as possible so all you have to do is throw the fish and shellfish into the tray.

✓ Other stuff
You can pick up samphire from most supermarket fish counters or greengrocers. Alternatively, use fennel fronds, dill, long chives or fine asparagus stems. If you use shelled raw prawns, add them halfway through as they won't need as long to cook.

Sumac Roast Chook with Nutty Wild Rice & a Honey Dressing

Isn't roast chicken clever? It never disappoints and needs very little doing to it. This is a warm North African version that steps up as a family meal fit for sharing. Leftovers make a great chicken and rice salad.

For 6
Prep time... 20 mins
Cook time... 2 hours

All you need is...

1.5–1.75kg whole chicken
1–2 tbsp olive oil
2 tsp sumac (it's in the spice section)
1 lemon

Rice
250g basmati and wild rice mix
1 red onion, peeled and finely chopped
2 tbsp olive oil
400g tin chickpeas, drained
100g pack roasted chopped hazelnuts
100g young leaf spinach

Dressing
200g natural yogurt
2 tbsp tahini
2 tsp runny honey

All you do is...

1 For the chook; preheat the oven to 180°C (fan), 200°C, gas mark 6. Pop the chicken into a roasting tin and pat the skin dry with kitchen paper. Drizzle over some olive oil then rub the sumac all over it and season. Cut the lemon in half, squeeze the juice into the cavity and pop in the lemon halves. Cover the top of the chicken with foil. Roast till the juices run clear (test the thigh), about 1 hour 15 minutes–1 hour 40 minutes, depending on the size of the chook (45 minutes per kilo, plus 20 minutes). Take off the foil for the last 20 minutes of the cooking time. Remove to a board and leave to rest for 10–15 minutes.

2 For the rice; cook it in plenty of boiling salted water for 15 minutes and drain. Meanwhile, in a deep frying pan, cook the onion in the olive oil for 5–10 minutes till it starts to caramelise. Add the chickpeas for another 5 minutes so the outsides start to go golden and nutty, then add the hazelnuts. Season and stir in the spinach for just a minute to slightly wilt, then add the cooked rice. Toss together.

3 For the yogurt sauce, just mix the ingredients in a small bowl with some pepper.

To serve
Skim the excess fat off the chicken juices in the oven tray then stir the meat juices into the rice. Carve and serve your chook on a bed of rice with plenty of dressing drizzled over.

Chuck-it-in Chopped Salad

Chop up all your favourite things, bung into a bowl along with the knobbly bits at the bottom of the veg tray and voilà. There's not much you can't put in so do improvise, but this combo is heavenly.

For 4
Prep time... 15 mins
Cook time... 5 mins

All you need is...

1 French baguette
2 tbsp olive oil
2 baby gem lettuce
1 large courgette, diced
100g cherry tomatoes, halved
20g fresh chives, finely chopped
1 red pepper, deseeded and diced
400g tin black beans, rinsed and
    drained
100g frozen sweetcorn, cooked and
    drained
1 ripe avocado, flesh diced
80g pack cubed pancetta
200g shelled raw king prawns

Dressing

5 tbsp olive oil
1 tbsp white wine vinegar
2 heaped tsp Dijon mustard

All you do is...

1 Preheat the oven to 160°C (fan), 180°C, gas mark 4. Tear up the baguette into a bowl then toss in the olive oil. Spread out the bread chunks in a roasting tin and pop in the oven for 10 minutes till golden. Set aside.

2 Dice the baby gems into a large bowl. Add the diced courgette, cherry tomato halves, chopped chives, diced pepper, black beans, cooked sweetcorn and avocado.

3 In a non-stick frying pan, cook the pancetta for 2 minutes then add the prawns for a further 2–3 minutes, stirring till cooked through.

4 Make the dressing by whisking all the ingredients together, season and toss it through the bowl of chopped salad.

To serve

Empty the bowl onto a really large plate and scatter over the croutons, prawns and pancetta.

Beef Ropa Vieja with Creamy Polenta

For 6–8
Prep time... 15 mins
Cook time... 3 hours 15 mins
(plus resting)
❄ (Beef only)

Zoe, my most lovely friend and, here's the bonus ball, my hairdresser, has been coming round to my house for years to blow, bouffé and beehive me. She is Cuban and proud of her country and cuisine, so when we are waiting for my colour to set or curlers to heat I get her to show me how her family feasts. 'Ropa Vieja', which means old clothes, is a classic Cuban family lunch. It literally melts in the mouth. She serves it with creamy polenta but rice is just as authentic. If you have any leftovers, just shred the meat into its rich sauce and have it as an exceptionally good ragu pasta sauce the next day.

All you need is...

2 tbsp olive oil
1.5kg piece of beef chunk or flank, tied with string
1 onion, peeled and chopped
1 celery stick, chopped
1 carrot, peeled and chopped
2 green peppers, deseeded and chopped
5 garlic cloves, peeled and crushed
2 tsp sweet smoked paprika
200ml hot beef stock
100ml tomato purée
2 x 400g tins chopped tomatoes
30g bunch of fresh coriander, chopped

All you do is...

1 Preheat the oven to 150°C (fan), 170°C, gas mark 3.

2 In a large heavy-based, flameproof and ovenproof dish set over a high heat, heat a tablespoon of olive oil then brown the beef joint on all sides. Remove the beef and add another tablespoon of olive oil, throwing in the onion, celery and carrot to soften for 5 minutes. Next, add the chopped green peppers and fry for another couple of minutes, followed by the crushed garlic and paprika for a further minute or so.

3 Add the hot stock, tomato purée and chopped tomatoes. Season, stir and bring to the boil. Place the beef joint back into the dish and cover with the sauce.

4 Pop on a lid and cook in the oven for 3 hours. Remove and rest for 10 minutes.

To serve
Carve into slices and serve on top of creamy polenta with the coriander scattered over.

Creamy Polenta

All you need is...

150g dried instant polenta
1 litre hot chicken stock
30g Parmesan, finely grated
a good knob of butter
1 tbsp crème fraîche

All you do is...

1 In a large pan, whisk the polenta and hot stock together, letting it bubble and cook for 5 minutes. Stir in the Parmesan cheese and butter to melt.

2 Stir through the crème fraîche and serve.

✓ De-stress
Make the beef day before, as the flavour is even better.

Whole Roast Colly with a Lemon Parmesan Dressing

Carve this at the table and serve it as a dramatic accompaniment to your Sunday roast or stew. It also works brilliantly as a meat-free centrepiece. Cauliflower is making a comeback.

For 4–6 (side) or 2 (main)
Prep time... 5 mins
Cook time... 30 mins

All you need is...

1 vegetable stock cube
1 whole large cauliflower, leaves peeled off
6 tbsp olive oil
3 big tbsp finely grated Parmesan
2 tbsp breadcrumbs
2 lemons

All you do is...

1 Preheat the oven to 200°C (fan), 220°C, gas mark 7. Dissolve the stock cube in 500ml boiling water. Put the cauliflower in a large pan, add the stock and top up to a ¼ of the way up the cauliflower with more boiling water. Put a lid on and simmer for 15 minutes. Remove and pop into an ovenproof dish.

2 Brush the outside of the cauliflower with 1 tablespoon of oil. In a small bowl, mix 1 tablespoon of oil and 1 tablespoon Parmesan with the breadcrumbs and the zest of 1 lemon. Now cover the top of the cauliflower with the mixed crumbs, gently pressing them on. Bake for 15 minutes till the topping is golden.

3 For the dressing, whisk the remaining 4 tablespoons olive oil with the remaining 2 tablespoons Parmesan and the juice from the 2 lemons and a grind of pepper.

To serve
Serve the whole baked cauliflower warm or at room temperature with the dressing on the side ready to pour over.

✓ De-stress
Make it a couple of hours before you sit down so it's at room temperature.

Sweet Fresh Duck Salad

For 4–6
Prep time... 15 mins
Cook time... 1 hour 10 mins

A trendy restaurant down the road from my house serves this delicious dish, but because I'm too stingy to pay their prices I've copied it and created a sweet, fresh salad with a little kick to make at home. That way I don't need to feel so guilty about splashing out on new shoes/handbag/face-lift … Works as a starter or a main dish to dazzle.

All you need is...

4 duck legs
120g cashew nuts
200g radishes
6 spring onions
100g bag watercress
¼ medium watermelon (about 500g)
30g bunch fresh mint, leaves chopped

Dressing
juice of 2 limes
1 tsp finely grated fresh ginger
1 tbsp runny honey
1 tbsp dark soy
1 tbsp sweet chilli sauce

All you do is...

1 Preheat the oven to 200°C (fan), 220°C, gas mark 7. Put some crumpled foil on the base of an oven tray and pop the duck legs on top. Cook for 1 hour, then cool.

2 Roast the nuts in a small roasting tin for just 5–10 minutes (keep an eye on them), then roughly chop.

3 In a large serving bowl, grate or very finely slice the radishes and spring onions. Roughly chop the watercress and cut the melon into bite-sized chunks. Throw in the chopped mint.

4 Shred the duck off the bone with 2 forks, slicing up the crispy skin, and add everything to the salad. Mix the dressing ingredients together and toss through at the last minute with the nuts thrown over.

To serve
Great with a big bowl of prawn crackers or sweet potato wedges.

✓ De-stress
Cook and shred the duck a few hours before, and make the dressing in advance.

✓ Impress
Make some curly spring onion garnishes by placing very thin long lengths of spring onions in iced water until they curl.

Royal Britannia Roast Lamb with a Herby Bean Dressing

This wonderful roast is full of British flavour; the lamb, the broad beans and the mint make a magnificent trio and taking a great big platter to my table makes me go all nostalgic about the green green grass of home. For lunch or dinner this is memorable food.

For 6–8
Prep time... 25 mins (plus resting)
Cook time... 1 hour 10 mins–
1 hour 30 mins

All you need is...

1.5–1.7kg leg of lamb, bone removed and rolled (keep the bones if you can)
3 big garlic cloves, peeled and thinly sliced
1 tbsp olive oil
2 tsp ground cumin

Beans
25g bunch fresh mint
25g bunch fresh parsley
25g bunch fresh basil
750g frozen baby broad beans, podded
3 tbsp olive oil
juice of 2 lemons

All you do is...

1 Preheat the oven to 220°C (fan), 240°C, gas mark 9.

2 Make incisions all over the lamb with a small kitchen knife and push the slices of garlic into the holes. Rub the lamb all over with the olive oil then rub the cumin and plenty of salt and pepper into the flesh too. Sit it, on the lamb bones if you have them, in a large oven tray. Cook for 20 minutes then turn down the heat to 160°C (fan), 180°C, gas mark 4 and cook for a further 55 minutes–1 hour 10 minutes. Work out this second cooking time exactly by allowing 20 minutes per 500g of the raw weight, so for a 1.7kg joint it is 1 hour 8 minutes. Rest for 15 minutes.

3 For the beans, finely chop the mint, parsley and basil leaves. Add to the podded broad beans and dress with the olive oil and the lemon juice just before serving.

To serve
Cut thick slices of the lamb and place on a big plate with the juices poured over and the broad beans spooned down the middle, with your best roast potatoes, of course.

✓ De-stress
To pod the frozen broad beans just put them in a bowl, cover with boiling water and leave for 5 minutes. Drain. Then with your nail nick a hole in the top and gently squeeze out each bean. Discard the shell. This will take 20 minutes or so. I do it in front of the TV and get the kids to help. You can make this up to a day in advance but add the herbs just before serving.

✓ Impress
If you've opened a bottle of wine (red or white), add some to the pan juices and bubble for a few minutes before straining to make the juices go further.

Wasabi Sesame Tuna with Crispy Noodle Salad

Wasabi gives a proper kick to this nutty melt-in-the-mouth tuna and noodle dish. I love it for its healthy, fresh, modern flavours and its simplicity to prepare.

For 4
Prep time... 15 mins
Cook time... 20 mins

All you need is...

4 x 150g tuna steaks
2 tbsp light soy sauce
1 tsp finely grated ginger
60g sesame seeds
2 tsp wasabi paste
1 tbsp olive oil

All you do is...

1 In a shallow bowl, marinate the tuna in the soy sauce and ginger for 10 minutes on each side.

2 Put the sesame seeds in a large flat bowl.

3 Drain the tuna from the marinade and on one side of each tuna steak evenly spread ½ teaspoon of the wasabi paste using the back of a teaspoon. Press the fish into the sesame seeds to cover both sides.

3 Heat the oil in a large non-stick pan and fry the tuna for 1–2 minutes on each side. You just want to turn the seeds golden but leave the flesh pink as it will continue to cook. Slice.

Crispy Noodle Salad

All you need is...

3 nests dried wholemeal egg noodles
2 tbsp olive oil
½ x iceberg lettuce
200g radishes, trimmed
25g fresh mint leaves, chopped

Dressing
1 x 18g sachet miso soup mix
2 tbsp olive oil
juice of 1 large lemon

All you do is...

1 Break the noodle nests into small pieces and put in a medium pan. Pour over boiling water and cook for 2 minutes. Drain well.

2 Heat the oil in a large non-stick frying pan, throw in the cooked noodle pieces and leave them to get crispy before flipping over. Keep frying and flipping till most have crisped up, about 7–8 minutes. Drain on kitchen paper and leave to cool.

3 Meanwhile, thinly slice the iceberg, very thinly slice or grate the radishes and mix with the mint. Whisk the dressing ingredients together.

To serve
Toss the leaves, noodles and dressing and serve immediately with your sliced tuna on top.

✓ De-stress
Coat the tuna beforehand. This works with white plain noodles too.

Speedy Horseradish Soda Bread

Fantastic to show off with, just don't tell anyone it only took 5 minutes to prepare. Couple with fish, chicken, beef, salads, soups … the list of bedfellows for this sexy loaf is endless.

For 6
Prep time... 5 mins
Cook time... 35 mins
❄

All you need is...

284ml carton buttermilk
2 tbsp creamed horseradish
   (from a jar)
150g wholemeal plain flour, sifted
1 tsp bicarbonate of soda
1 tsp salt
2 tsp soft light brown sugar
150g plain flour, sifted, plus extra
   for sprinkling

All you do is...

1 Preheat the oven to 180°C (fan), 200°C, gas mark 6.

2 In a large bowl, mix the buttermilk and horseradish. Add the wholemeal flour, bicarbonate of soda, salt and sugar. Finally, add the plain flour, mix together briefly with a cutlery knife and then with your hands, and gently bring the dough together.

3 It will be a little sticky, but shape the dough into a rough round loaf about 18cm across and pop it on a well-floured oven tray. Mark a deep cross in it with a sharp, serrated knife. Sprinkle with a little extra flour on top and bake for 30–35 minutes. Rest for at least 10 minutes before cutting into it.

✓ De-stress
Make it beforehand and warm through in the oven. This loaf freezes really well.

✓ Impress
If you haven't got buttermilk make your own by adding 1 tablespoon lemon juice or cider vinegar to 275ml milk and leave for 5 minutes before using.

Baked Tahini Salmon

For 6–10
Prep time... 5 mins
Cook time... 15–30 mins

This is seriously easy to prepare but so impressive on the table. It's perfect to feed a big crowd, so try serving it cold with salads and breads as a fabulous picnic showpiece. Or serve it hot or cold for lunch or dinner. It's my go-to for summer Saturdays with friends. Try it with Speedy Horseradish Soda Bread (see p84) and roasted asparagus.

All you need is...

1 whole side of salmon fillet (sizes vary, see below for cooking times), approx 800g–1.2kg
1 heaped tbsp light tahini (sesame seed paste)
200g thick authentic Greek yogurt
2 tbsp lemon juice

To serve

15g fresh mint leaves, finely chopped
15g fresh flat-leaf parsley leaves, finely chopped
50g pine nuts, toasted

All you do is...

1 Preheat the oven to 200°C (fan), 220°C, gas mark 7.

2 Lay the fillet, skin side down, on a foil-lined baking tray and season.

3 Mix the tahini, yogurt and lemon juice in a small bowl with some seasoning and spread it over the top of the fish. Work out the cooking time, based on 5 minutes per 200g of fish, so between 15–30 minutes. For an 800g fillet, the time will be 20 minutes. When cooked it should be slightly pink in the middle.

To serve

Scatter the mint, parsley and pine nuts over the whole fish.

✓ De-stress
If feeding a crowd, just increase the topping when using more fish.

Sweetcorn & Mint Fritters with Griddled Halloumi

A great balance of sweet and salty flavours that uses up that bag of sweetcorn you'd forgotten you had in the back of the freezer. Be generous with the sweet chilli sauce and don't forget to buy more sweetcorn for the next lot of fritters.

For 4
Prep time... 10 mins
Cook time... 15 mins
❄ (fritters only)

All you need is...

350g frozen sweetcorn
100g plain flour
1 tsp baking powder
½ tsp ground cumin
3 large eggs
3 salad onions, finely chopped
10g fresh mint leaves, chopped
3 tbsp olive oil
250g halloumi
sweet chilli sauce, to serve

All you do is...

1 Put the sweetcorn in a large bowl and pour over boiling water to defrost. Cover and leave for 5–10 minutes. Drain.

2 To make the batter, place the flour, baking powder and cumin together in a large bowl and whisk in the eggs until smooth. Season. Now thoroughly mix in the salad onions, chopped mint and drained sweetcorn.

3 Heat 1 tablespoon of oil in a large non-stick frying pan then ladle in 4 rounds of the mixture (half of the batter) and fry for 2–3 minutes on each side. Remove, cover, and repeat using another tablespoon of oil with the rest of the batter to make 8 fritters in total. Set aside and keep warm while you fry the cheese.

4 Slice the halloumi into 8 slices and brush with the remaining olive oil on both sides. Preheat a griddle or use the non-stick frying pan and fry the cheese for 1–2 minutes on each side till charred.

To serve

Stack 2 fritters and 2 slices of halloumi per portion on plates. Finish with a drizzle of sweet chilli sauce on each.

✓ De-stress
If pushed for time, cook the fritters a few hours ahead and reheat in a low oven – you have a meal in minutes!

Sweet Magic Kale

For 4
Prep time... 5 mins
Cook time... 15 mins

Once upon a time I was scared of kale, then a handsome prince in a delivery van substituted my spinach for this wrinkly green monster. To my surprise I have fallen under its spell. Sweet, earthy and full of good stuff, pair it with Indian flavours, roasts, fish or lamb. It definitely delivers a happy ending.

All you need is...

1 tbsp extra virgin olive oil
1 red onion, peeled and finely sliced
2 garlic cloves, peeled and crushed
50g sultanas
200g curly leaf kale, trimmed of
    big stems
½ tbsp sherry vinegar
50g pine nuts, toasted

All you do is...

1 Heat the oil in a large, deep, non-stick frying pan. Add the onion and cook for about 10 minutes till just starting to caramelise at the edges. Add the garlic, stirring for 1 minute, then the sultanas, and toss together.

2 Now throw in the kale and cook for about 5 minutes, turning it over every now and then.

3 When tender but not soggy, dress with the sherry vinegar and pine nuts. Season and serve.

Italian Holiday Schnitzel with Aglio e Olio

For 4
Prep time... 10 mins (plus chilling)
Cook time... 10 mins

Visiting the in-laws conjures up visions of grey meat and two veg, padded toilet seats and an atmosphere you could cut with a butter knife. Well, luckily for me my in-laws are nestled on the side of a Tuscan mountain bejewelled with olive groves and a proper guest bed. They make their own olive oil, harvest their own tomatoes and know the name of the chicken they're eating. This is the meal we always arrive to and the one the kids ask me for daily on our return. Smug? Me? No. Just grateful for small culinary mercies.

All you need is...

2 big skinless chicken breasts (about 175g each)
100g tomato purée
4 tbsp olive oil
100g fresh breadcrumbs
2 fresh rosemary sprigs, leaves finely chopped

All you do is...

1 Halve the chicken breasts horizontally and bash them down between sheets of cling film into thin slices.

2 Mix the tomato purée with 2 tablespoons olive oil in a large wide bowl. In a separate wide bowl, mix the breadcrumbs and chopped rosemary together. Season.

3 Now smear the tomato mix all over the thin chicken pieces then press into the breadcrumbs until completely coated. Cover and pop in the fridge till needed.

4 Heat 1 tablespoon of olive oil in a large non-stick frying pan over a medium–high heat and fry 2 of the schnitzels for 2–3 minutes on each side until golden, crispy and completely cooked through. Use another tablespoon of oil for the rest of the chicken. Drain on kitchen paper and serve or keep warm in the oven while you knock up the pasta.

Aglio e Olio

All you need is...

400g dried spaghetti
4 tbsp olive oil
3 garlic cloves, peeled and crushed
a pinch of dried chilli flakes
2 tbsp chopped fresh parsley
1 lemon, cut into wedges
30g Parmesan, finely grated

All you do is...

1 Cook the spaghetti as per the pack instructions, then drain.

2 Meanwhile, heat the olive oil in a large pan and gently fry the crushed garlic for 1 minute till just golden, adding the dried chilli for a few seconds at the end. Throw in the cooked pasta and toss thoroughly, adding the chopped parsley to finish.

To serve
Serve with lemon wedges and grated Parmesan and top with the chicken.

✓ De-stress
Whizz the rosemary leaves with the breadcrumbs in a food processor.
✓ Impress
Make this a posh chicken burger in a bun with plenty of mayo and salad.

Mexican Chicken Soup with Salsa & Corn Chips

Fresh, light and tasty, the lime and tomato salsa lifts this sweet, hot soup into my top 10. Insist on a Mexican wave when the bowls are empty … 'cos they will be.

For 4
Prep time... 15 mins
Cook time... 15 mins

All you need is...

1 tbsp olive oil
1 red onion, peeled and finely chopped
2 garlic cloves, peeled and crushed
1 tsp smoked paprika
1 tsp ground cumin
400g tin chopped tomatoes
2 tbsp tomato purée
1 tbsp runny honey
1 litre hot chicken stock
2 skinless chicken breasts
100g baby spinach
80g Cheddar, grated
150g bag corn chips

Salsa

1 ripe avocado
3 tomatoes
3 spring onions
½ medium hot chilli, deseeded and chopped
juice of 1 lime
handful of fresh coriander, chopped

All you do is...

1 Heat the olive oil in a large pan and fry the red onion for 5 minutes till soft. Add the garlic for a minute more then the paprika and cumin. Stir for another minute or so then add the tinned tomatoes, tomato purée, honey and hot stock. Season and stir.

2 Very thinly slice the chicken breasts and add to the soup. Let it bubble away for 10 minutes until the chicken is completely cooked.

3 Meanwhile, make the salsa. Peel, stone and roughly chop the avocado flesh, then chop the tomatoes and spring onions. Pop in a bowl with the chilli, lime juice and coriander.

4 Take the soup off the heat and stir through the baby spinach leaves.

To serve

Fill the bowls with the chicken soup, add a spoonful of salsa on top, followed by some grated cheese. Scatter a few corn chips over and have the rest on the side to dip into.

✓ De-stress
If the coriander is a no-no then swap for mint, and if chilli is a challenge, just leave it out.

Creamy Salmon & Leek Lasagne

For 4–6
Prep time... 20 mins
Cook time... 50 mins

My favourite easy lunch-party oven dish, I've cut out all the long-winded bits of making a traditional lasagne and replaced it with creamy subtle flavours that need very little preparation. The result is impressive, guaranteeing that all age groups come back for seconds.

All you need is...

2 tbsp olive oil
400g leeks, trimmed and finely chopped
150g frozen chopped spinach
10g fresh dill, fronds finely chopped
300ml half-fat crème fraîche
150g pack Boursin soft garlic cheese
200ml hot chicken stock
250–300g pack fresh lasagne sheets
400g raw salmon fillet, skinned and thinly sliced
125g ball mozzarella cheese, drained and torn

All you do is...

1 Preheat the oven to 180°C (fan), 200°C, gas mark 6.

2 Heat the oil in a large non-stick frying pan and cook the leeks for 5 minutes till softened. Add the frozen spinach and melt it down with the leeks, then add the chopped dill and stir. Season and set aside.

3 In a large bowl, gently whisk together the crème fraîche, boursin and stock till combined and smooth.

4 In an ovenproof dish, 22 x 26cm, assemble the lasagne in these layers: first the spinach and leek, second the salmon, third the spinach and leek, putting two sheets of pasta, side-by-side, between each layer. Start with the sauce and distribute it evenly throughout. Finish with a layer of pasta, a couple of spoons of the sauce and tear the mozzarella over the top.

5 Place the dish on a baking tray and bake for 40–50 minutes till bubbling and golden on top. Rest for 5–10 minutes before serving.

To serve
Serve with baby spinach leaves dressed with olive oil and lemon juice.

✓ De-stress
This is a great one to assemble the night before and bake when you are ready – add 15 minutes to the cook time.

'If you really want to make
a friend, go to someone's
house and eat with him ...
the people who give you their
food give you their heart.'
Cesar Chavez

Smoked salmon brioche mouthfuls

Sesame prawn toasts

Antipasti sharing plate

Parce the Spanish parcels

San choy bau

Scandi sharing plate

Sushi bites – mackerel & horseradish, & wasabi avocado

bite-size

Smoked Salmon Brioche Mouthfuls

Makes 60 canapé size
Prep time... 15 mins
Cook time... 5 mins

I hate the canapé thing. Is it a starter? Will I get fed properly later? Have I got half of it left in my teeth and how do I not look greedy when a good lot go past and I rugby tackle the waiter to the ground? Well, these are melt-in-the-mouth good, but have style and substance. I use them for drinks parties, as a starter, posh picnics and birthday breakfasts … but do watch out for the caviar in your teeth!

All you need is...

1 pack of 10 brioche rolls
300g smoked salmon
300ml tub half-fat crème fraîche
50g pot black lumpfish caviar
1 small bunch fresh chives, finely
  chopped
1 lemon, cut into wedges

All you do is...

1 Preheat the grill to medium. Cut each brioche roll thickly into 6 round slices. Toast both sides under the grill (watch them as they go quick).

2 Lay the toasts out on a big plate, board or tray. Divide the salmon among the toasted brioche rounds and dollop each with ½ teaspoon of crème fraîche.

3 Add a smidge of caviar, scatter the chives over the lot, then a grind of pepper to finish.

To serve
Serve with lemon wedges to squeeze over.

✓ De-stress
Toast the bases in advance and reheat in a low oven when ready to assemble.

Sesame Prawn Toasts

For 4–6
Prep time... 10 mins
Cook time... 5 mins

Growing up, there was only one restaurant in our suburban high street to go to for fancy grub. The Good Earth – a really posh Chinese right next door to the ladies' hosiery shop where I bought my first bra. Back then, fried prawn toasts were an exotic treat and although my bra size has changed, my love of these bite-sized Oriental morsels has not. So here's my healthy modern version fit for a finger food feast.

All you need is...

2 tbsp sesame seeds
4 tbsp olive oil
6 medium slices white loaf,
    crusts cut off
175g cooked small prawns
1 tsp finely grated fresh ginger
1 tbsp light soy sauce
juice of ½ lemon

All you do is...

1 Toast the sesame seeds in a large non-stick frying pan stirring constantly (watch them, they only take a minute). Set aside.

2 In the same pan, add half the oil to heat then fry half the bread slices on both sides till golden. Do the same with the other half. Cut each slice into quarters to make small triangles.

3 For the topping, in a food processor whizz the prawns, ginger, soy sauce and lemon juice (or very finely chop if you don't have a food processor).

4 To assemble, just divide the prawn mix and spread onto the triangle toasts then sprinkle with the toasted sesame seeds.

To serve
Serve on a big plate for greedy fingers to grab at.

✓ Impress
Serve with ribbons of cucumber to garnish.

Antipasti Sharing Plate

For 6–8 (starter)
Prep time... 10 mins
Cook time... 20 mins (plus cooling)

I'm usually too focused on pudding to think about a starter, frankly, but if I do want to give my friends something before the main dish I need it to be low maintenance but delicious. This is a classic Italian combination spread out on your favourite board or tray that you can leave for everyone to unceremoniously tuck into. Perfect for drinks, dinner parties or lunches with family, most of it's out of a packet, but no one seems to notice …

All you need is...

2 long red peppers, halved and deseeded
1 tbsp extra virgin olive oil, plus 100ml for dipping
8 small figs
4 ripe vine-tomatoes, roughly chopped
150g salami, sliced in half
150g Parma or Serrano ham
125g ball buffalo mozzarella
400g sourdough loaf, warmed, to serve
1 tsp balsamic vinegar
1 tbsp sea salt flakes
200g anchovy stuffed olives
a few fresh basil leaves

All you do is...

1 Preheat the oven to 180°C (fan), 200°C, gas mark 6. Place the pepper halves in a small roasting tray and drizzle with 1 tablespoon olive oil. Season and roast for 20 minutes. Leave to cool then thickly slice.

2 Cut the figs into quarters leaving them still attached at the base. Gently open out each of the figs by squeezing them from the base. Roughly cut the tomatoes into small chunks.

To serve

Lay everything out on a really big plate, wooden board or tray, roughly grouping together each ingredient. Arrange the cooked meats at one end in folds, then group together the chopped tomatoes and pepper slices. Tear the mozzarella on and add the bread. Pour olive oil into a small bowl with a drop of balsamic vinegar in the middle. Put the sea salt in a small bowl and use another for the olives. Place the figs on randomly and tear the basil over the tomatoes and mozzarella. Lastly, drizzle with olive oil and a twist of black pepper.

✓ De-stress
Precook the peppers then all you have to do is plate up.

Parce the Spanish Parcels

Like little calzone these are bursting with flavour; pile them up high on a big plate for parties or picnics. These are also delicious as a midweek tea, just use halve the mixture, only one roll of pastry, then pop the leftover tomato and chorizo sauce on top of jacket potatoes or pasta the next day.

For 16 parcels
Prep time... 20 mins
Cook time... 45 mins
❄

All you need is...

1–2 x 320g packs ready rolled
    shortcrust pastry
a splash of olive oil
1 red onion, peeled and
    finely chopped
100g chorizo, finely diced
400g tin chickpeas, drained
400g tin chopped tomatoes
125g ball mozzarella, drained
    and finely diced
1 egg, beaten

All you do is...

1 Take the pastry out of the fridge 20 minutes before using. Preheat the oven to 200°C (fan), 220°C, gas mark 7.

2 Heat the oil in a frying pan and cook the onion and chorizo for 5 minutes till they start to caramelise. Add the chickpeas for another 5 minutes before pouring in the tomatoes. Simmer for 5 more minutes before removing from the heat and stirring in the mozzarella pieces. Take off the heat and leave the filling to cool.

3 Unroll the pastry and cut down the middle lengthways then cut each half into 4, creating 8 equal rectangles. (Repeat with the second roll if using).

4 Divide the chorizo mix equally among the rectangles (about 2 loaded teaspoons per parcel), folding the pastry over the filling in the middle. Use a fork to press down around the open edges.

5 Place the parcels on 1–2 lined baking trays, brush each with egg to glaze and cut a small steam hole in the top with the tip of a sharp knife. Bake for 25–30 minutes till golden.

To serve
Serve warm or at room temperature.

✓ De-stress
Make the filling the day before.

San Choy Bau

For 4–6 (or as a main course for 4
with Crispy Noodle Salad (see p83)
Prep time... 10 mins
Cook time... 15 mins

When Dan and I were young and trendy living in a cool part of town we lived off this dish. It's a sharing plate, a starter or a main served with a Crispy Noodle Salad (see p83). That savoury pork mince with cool, crisp lettuce offers a surprise with every bite. Now we've moved to the sensible side of the street and are no longer too cool for school, but we still love San Choy Bau.

All you need is...

2 tbsp peanut oil
500g pork mince
2 red peppers, deseeded
    and chopped
6 salad onions, trimmed and chopped
2 garlic cloves, peeled and crushed
2 tsp freshly grated ginger
2 tbsp light soy sauce
2 tbsp hoisin sauce
3 baby gem lettuces, leaves
    separated and washed

All you do is...

1 Over a high heat, heat the oil in a large non-stick frying pan or wok and fry the mince for 5 minutes, turning it and breaking it up as it browns.

2 Add the peppers and onions and cook for another 5 minutes. Then add the garlic. Keep stirring the meat for a further 2 minutes then add the ginger, soy and hoisin sauces. Stir to coat for another 2 minutes.

To serve
Spoon the pork mix into the whole baby leaves and serve on a big plate for all to tuck into.

Scandi Sharing Plate

For 4
Prep time... 30 mins
(plus 1 hour standing)
Cook time... 10 mins

I thought Dan would book a weekend in Paris, Venice or even New York for our 10th anniversary, but to my slightly spoilt horror he surprised me with ... Copenhagen. (Fay stamps foot and pouts). However, we had a wonderful couple of days filled with some of the most memorable morsels that Scandinavia has to offer. This fashionable plate reminds me of that brilliant city and is perfect for picking at with friends, coupled with vodka or a crisp white wine. I wonder where we'll go for our 20th?

All you need is...

1 whole cucumber
1 tbsp caster sugar
1 tbsp white wine vinegar
150g smoked trout
2 tbsp natural yogurt
2 tbsp cream cheese
1 tbsp roughly chopped fresh
　dill leaves
260g rollmop herrings, drained
4 slices German rye bread
1 small fennel, very finely sliced
120g smoked salmon
1 lemon, to serve

All you do is...

1 For the pickled cucumber, very finely slice the cucumber and put it in a bowl with the sugar and vinegar. Add a good pinch of salt. Stir vigorously and leave for at least an hour or overnight covered in the fridge (you could use a clean jam jar and give it a good shake).

2 For the smoked trout pâté, break up the trout into a food processor along with the yogurt, cream cheese, dill leaves and some black pepper. Whizz till smooth and pop in a small bowl.

3 Unroll the rollmops and slice into long thin slivers; reserve the onions.

4 Toast the rye bread (this needs toasting and cooling twice to make it crispy) and cut each piece into 4.

To serve
To assemble, just drain the cucumber and put it in a small bowl on a large plate or board. Add the bowl of trout pâté, the sliced rollmops with the onions sprinkled over, a pile of sliced fennel, the smoked salmon and the rye toasts. Quarter the lemon and nuzzle into the gaps, then finish with a good grinding of black pepper all over.

Sushi Bites – Mackerel & Horseradish, & Wasabi Avocado

These mouthfuls are perfect finger food. Most supermarkets stock a wide range of global products you can get creative with the flavour combos. Try duck and hoisin or smoked salmon and pickled cucumber. I always say that food calories don't count if there's seaweed in it, so happy healthy nibbling.

For 48 bites (24 of each)
Prep time... 25 mins
Cook time... 15 mins

All you need is...

200g sushi rice (or basmati rice)
3 tsp rice vinegar
3 sheets nori seaweed
    (½ x 17g pack)
2 x 100g smoked mackerel fillets,
    skinned
6 tbsp mayo
3 tsp creamed horseradish
2 ripe avocados, halved and stoned
3 tsp wasabi paste
3 tsp black seeds (sesame or onion)

All you do is...

1 Cook the sushi rice as per the pack instructions then leave to steam for 5 minutes longer than suggested to get sticky and overcooked. Mix in the rice vinegar and spread onto a plate to cool completely.

2 Cut the nori sheets into squares of about 5cm – there will be 48. Lay them out in batches on a board as they're assembled. Push a teaspoon of rice onto the middle of each one followed by your topping...

3 For the Mackerel Sushi: Pull off bite-sized pieces of fish and pop them on the rice, then mix 3 tablespoons of mayo with the horseradish and squeeze a blob on each.

4 For the Avocado Sushi: Slice the avocados into small pieces and pop a piece on each of the rice parcels. Then mix 3 tablespoons of mayo with the wasabi paste and dollop a blob on each.

To serve
Sprinkle with the black seeds.

✓ De-stress
The easiest way to put the mayo on top is to fill the corner of a small food bag and snip a tiny hole to pipe it on. Mix the mayo in advance, snip the sheets and assemble at the last minute.

'Since Eve ate apples, much
depends on dinner.'
Lord Byron

delish
dinners

delish dinners

Slow-cook
So-good
Beef Stew

For 4
Prep time... 15 mins
Cook time... 2 hours 15 mins
❄

This is a recipe that allows you to get on with life. While this rich, warm, winter stew simmers away in your oven you can plan a holiday, de-scale the kettle and colour code your Tupperware. It's even better the next day, and if there are leftovers, just pop a pastry lid on for the best pie filling ever.

All you need is...

2 tbsp olive oil
600g braising or stewing beef, diced
2 red onions, peeled
    and roughly chopped
6 rashers smoked streaky bacon,
    roughly chopped
250g large mushrooms,
    roughly chopped
5 medium carrots, peeled
    and quartered
100ml red wine
500ml beef stock
1 tbsp Worcestershire sauce
2 tbsp tomato purée

All you do is...

1 Preheat the oven to 160°C (fan), 180°C, gas mark 4.

2 Heat a tablespoon of olive oil in a large heavy-based, flameproof and ovenproof dish over a medium–high heat. Season the beef then, in batches, cook the meat till brown all over, about 5 minutes. Set aside.

3 Add another tablespoon of olive oil to the dish along with the onions and bacon and cook for 5 minutes.

4 Throw in the chopped mushrooms and big bits of carrot and cook for another 2–3 minutes. Then pour in the wine to bubble and burn off for another 5 minutes. Add the stock, Worcestershire sauce and tomato purée, then add the browned beef and stir. Bring to the boil, cover, then pop in the oven to cook for 2 hours.

To serve
Serve with mash and Purple-red Cabbage (see p151).

Prawn Pad Thai

Dinner in minutes that feels like a takeaway but is healthy, tasty and brilliant for all ages? Here you go ...

For 4
Prep time... 10 mins
Cook time... 10 mins

All you need is...

200g dried flat rice noodles
1 tbsp groundnut or olive oil
6 salad onions, chopped
125g Tenderstem broccoli tips, roughly chopped
2 garlic cloves, peeled and crushed
200g raw king prawns, shelled
2 eggs
1 tbsp light soy sauce
1 tbsp toasted sesame oil
1 dsp fish sauce
1 large carrot, peeled and grated
2 limes
100g salted peanuts
1 tbsp chopped fresh coriander, roughly chopped

All you do is...

1 Cook the noodles as per the pack instructions and drain.

2 In a wok or large frying pan, heat the groundnut or olive oil then fry the onions and broccoli for 2–3 minutes. Add the crushed garlic and prawns for 2–3 minutes till cooked through.

3 Now crack in the eggs and keep stirring for a minute to cook. Add the drained noodles, soy sauce, sesame oil and fish sauce.

4 Take off the heat and add the grated carrot and juice of 1 lime. Toss to combine.

5 Put the peanuts in a food bag and bash with a rolling pin to roughly break them up.

To serve
Pile the pad Thai into a large serving dish, scatter over the peanuts and coriander and serve with the extra lime cut into quarters on the side.

✓ Impress
Chopped fresh chilli is a great addition, as is a rose cut from a radish – but I'd forget the rose and put your feet up personally.

✓ De-stress
If coriander scares you, just swap it for fresh mint.

Patatas Bravas

A potato option that's easy, tasty and a little bit different. I pair it with so many things as a side dish or just tuck into a plateful with a fried egg on top for a stress-free supper.

For 4
Prep time... 10 mins
Cook time... 45 mins

All you need is...

2 tbsp olive oil

1kg potatoes, skin on

2 tsp smoked paprika

2 x 400g tins chopped tomatoes

2 tbsp tomato purée

3 garlic cloves, peeled and crushed

All you do is...

1 Preheat the oven to 200°C (fan), 220°C, gas mark 7 and preheat the oil in a roasting tray. Chop the potatoes into small bite-sized chunks.

2 Toss the potatoes in the hot oil then sprinkle with the smoked paprika. Stir thoroughly to coat and bake for 20 minutes.

3 In a bowl, mix the tinned tomatoes, tomato purée and garlic. After the first 20 minutes is up, stir the tomato sauce into the potatoes and pop back into the oven for another 25 minutes.

To serve
Serve with plain grilled meats, fish or vegetables.

...ne, Japanese understand this concept within another fo...
...land as "the pathos of things," mono no aware is the u...
...zens of life come right before the moment ends. In a full acc...

Salmon on Pancetta & Leek Mash

A great plate of flavours that simply works, it's as easy to eat as it is to prepare.

For 4
Prep time... 15 mins
Cook time... 25 mins

All you need is...

800g potatoes, peeled and cubed
3–4 tbsp olive oil
80g pack cubed pancetta
2 leeks, trimmed and finely sliced
3 tbsp vegetable stock (use ½ cube)
4 x 150g salmon fillets, skin on

All you do is...

1 Boil, drain, then mash the potatoes. While they are bubbling away, heat a large frying pan with 1 tablespoon olive oil and cook the pancetta and leeks for 10 minutes till soft and the pancetta starts to crisp.

2 When the spuds are mashed, throw in the cooked leeks, pancetta, stock and a good glug of olive oil. Mix well and season.

3 Using the same frying pan as for the pancetta, heat another tablespoon of olive oil in it and fry the fish fillets for 3–4 minutes on each side, skin side first, until just cooked through and the skin is crispy.

To serve
Lay the fish on top of a big spoonful of the savoury mash. It's great with a salad of baby spinach on the side.

✓ De-stress
Make the mash in advance and gently reheat, adding a little more of the stock.

✓ Impress
Garnish the plate with sizzled capers. Simply dry a small jar of drained capers on kitchen paper and fry in olive oil for a few minutes until crispy, then drain well. Serve the salmon with the crispy skin side up.

Chicken with Beans One-pot Wonder

Comfort food at its most cosy, this is a warming pot that makes me want to snuggle up in a tiger onesie with a box set of *The Galloping Gourmet*. Feel free to feed a crowd with your chicken and beans ... but only if they're all in onesies.

For 4
Prep time... 10 mins
Cook time... 40 mins

All you need is...

2 tbsp olive oil
8 big skinless, boneless chicken thighs
2 large leeks, trimmed and thinly
    sliced
1 tbsp fresh rosemary leaves,
    chopped
2 garlic cloves, peeled and crushed
120ml dry white wine
250ml chicken stock
2 tsp grainy mustard
2 x 400g tins flageolet beans, drained,
    but not rinsed
3 slices Serrano ham
handful of fresh flat-leaf parsley,
    leaves chopped

All you do is...

1 Heat half the olive oil in a heavy-based casserole dish or large non-stick pan. Brown the chicken thighs till the outside looks nutty all over. Remove and set aside.

2 Throw in the leeks with a second glug of oil. Soften for 2–3 minutes then add the rosemary and garlic for another minute.

3 Stir in the wine and let bubble for 2–3 minutes, stirring all the good stuff off the bottom of the pan Add the stock, mustard and beans, then tear in the ham.

4 Bring to the boil then lower the heat, pop a lid on and simmer for 25–30 minutes till the chicken is tender and cooked through. Throw in the parsley.

To serve
Serve with crusty wholemeal bread to soak up those juices.

✓ De-stress
Any tinned pulses work in this dish; whatever you have in the cupboard. Parma ham can replace the Serrano.

Sweet Miso Fish with Creamy Coconut Rice

This is moist melt-in-your-mouth cooking in minutes and will become one of your family favourites for sure. Serve it as a big Chinese feast with Crispy Sesame Kale (see p144), Soy Roast Colly (see p169), with Sesame Prawn Toasts to start (see p104) and a bowl of fortune cookies.

For 4
Prep time... 5 mins
Cook time... 10 mins

All you need is...

4 x 150g skinless fish fillets (haddock, cod and salmon work brilliantly)
3 tbsp mirin or dry sherry
1 tbsp light soy sauce
2 sachets miso paste

All you do is...

1 If you can, marinate the fish in the rest of the ingredients for a few hours in the fridge (it's a bonus but not essential).

2 Preheat the oven to 220°C (fan), 240°C, gas mark 9.

3 In a ceramic ovenproof dish bake the fish in the marinade for 10–12 minutes. Serve immediately.

Creamy Coconut Rice

For 4
Prep time... 5 mins
Cook time... 20 mins

All you need is...

250g white basmati rice, rinsed
200ml light coconut milk
1 tbsp desiccated coconut
juice of 1 lime

All you do is...

1 Put the rice in a pan with the coconut milk, coconut, a big pinch of salt and water to cover up to the first joint of your thumb (2.5cm above the rice). Bring to the boil, cover, then turn down the heat and simmer for 5 minutes. Turn off the heat and leave well alone for 10 minutes.

2 Stir through the lime juice and serve.

✓ De-stress
I like having the fish marinating in the fridge beforehand so that all I have to do is bung it in the oven at the last minute.

✓ Impress
Use a hand-held zester to take some zest off a lime, sprinkle over the rice and cut the lime into chunks to serve.

Fast Coconut & Lime Fish Curry

A quick recipe that delivers taste in lorry loads is worth its weight in gold. Well, here it is – a solid gold delicious creamy taste of Thailand in minutes.

For 4
Prep time...10 mins
Cook time...15 mins

All you need is...

100g blanched peanuts
1 garlic clove, peeled and crushed
160ml tin coconut cream
1 tbsp light soy sauce
1 tbsp fish sauce
zest and juice of 1 lime, plus wedges
    to serve
½–1 red chilli (to taste), deseeded
    and chopped
500g river cobbler, cod loin or
    haddock, skinned and boned
250g raw peeled king prawns
10g fresh coriander, roughly chopped

All you do is...

1 Preheat the oven to 200°C (fan), 220°C, gas mark 7. Roast the peanuts on an oven tray for 5–10 minutes (watch them!). Grind the roasted peanuts in a food processer to fine crumbs then add the garlic, coconut cream, soy sauce, fish sauce, lime zest and juice and chilli.

2 Cut the fish into bite-sized chunks and spread out in a large, shallow oven dish along with the prawns. Pour over the sauce, stir to coat and bake for 15–18 minutes till the fish is cooked through. Serve scattered with the coriander and lime wedges.

To serve
Great with steamed rice.

✓ De-stress
If you don't have a food processor just bash the nuts in a food bag then use a hand blender to whizz up the sauce.
✓ Impress
Toast coconut flesh by very thinly slicing with a veg peeler and roasting in the oven.

Baked BBQ Bangers with Apple Mash

Sausages cut through class, age and fashion. These are smoky snags with an earthy apple mash that balances the sweetness of the sauce – a people pleaser.

For 4–6
Prep time... 25 mins
Cook time... 50 mins

All you need is...

8-12 fat sausages
1 tbsp olive oil, plus 1 tsp
1 red onion, peeled and finely
  chopped
1 tsp smoked paprika
2 tbsp tomato ketchup
1 tbsp Worcestershire sauce
1 tsp Dijon mustard
2 tbsp apple juice
1 tbsp balsamic vinegar
½ red chilli, deseeded and
  roughly chopped (optional)

All you do is...

1 Preheat the oven to 160°C (fan), 180°C, gas mark 4.

2 Put the sausages in a non-stick roasting tin and coat them with the teaspoon of olive oil. Roast the sausages for 40 minutes, gently shaking the tin occasionally.

3 Meanwhile, fry the onion in the 1 tablespoon olive oil in a non-stick frying pan for 5–7 minutes till soft. Add the smoked paprika and stir over the heat for a minute. Now whizz with a hand blender or transfer to a food processor, adding the tomato ketchup, Worcestershire sauce, mustard, apple juice, vinegar and chilli (if using) till smoothish.

4 Smother the browned sausages with the sauce and roast for another 10–15 minutes until glazed.

To serve
Serve with the mash (overleaf).

✓ De-stress
Make the sauce a couple of days in advance, and keep in the fridge.
✓ Impress
Make extra sauce and give little jars of the stuff to your mates as a pressie (this recipe makes 180g, so would be easy to make in larger batches). Try replacing the apple juice with Bourbon for an adult kick.

Potato and Apple 'Heaven & Earth' Mash

All you need is...

1kg potatoes, peeled and quartered
2 tbsp olive oil
a squirt of runny honey
2 eating apples, peeled and grated

All you do is...

1 Place the potatoes in a large pan of cold salted water and bring to the boil. Lower the heat and cook for 20 minutes until tender. Drain and steam-dry in the colander for 5 minutes.

2 Mash with a potato ricer (preferably) or potato masher. Stir in the olive oil, honey and grated apples with some seasoning. Stir the potatoes over a gentle heat for a few minutes to soften the apples.

To serve
Serve piles of mash with the bbq sausages and some greens.

Steak with a Red Wine & Rosemary Sauce & Rough Rustic Roasties

Proper food to impress and no messing about, just classic flavours. Serve with a green salad tossed in a mustard dressing.

For 4
Prep time... 15 mins
Cook time... 50 mins

All you need is...

1 tbsp olive oil
4 x 250–300g sirloin steaks (about 2cm thick), at room temperature
2 tbsp fresh rosemary sprigs, leaves finely chopped
2 garlic cloves, peeled and crushed
50g butter
4 anchovy fillets, roughly chopped
200ml red wine
150ml beef stock
1 tbsp Worcestershire sauce

All you do is...

1 Rub the olive oil all over the steaks, season them and preheat a non-stick frying pan until very hot. Sear the steaks for 1–2 minutes on each side depending on the thickness of the meat.

2 Remove and cover with foil. Lower the heat.

3 In the same pan, stir-fry the rosemary for 1 minute then stir in the garlic for another minute. Now melt the butter until it turns frothy. Add the chopped anchovies and keep stirring until they melt.

4 Pour in the red wine and turn the heat up to a strong bubble for 5 minutes. Add the stock and Worcestershire sauce and let bubble and reduce to a thick pouring consistency, about 5 minutes.

5 Pour any extra juice from the steaks into the sauce. Serve each steak drizzled with the sauce and the rustic roasties on the side.

Rough Rustic Roasties

All you need is...

2 tbsp olive oil
1kg potatoes (Maris Piper or similar), skins on

All you do is...

1 Preheat the oven to 200°C (fan), 220°C, gas mark 7. Heat the oil in a large roasting tray.

2 Chop the potatoes into even-sized chunks and parboil for 10 minutes till just cooked through. Drain and leave them to dry for 5 minutes in the colander.

3 Now toss the potatoes in the hot oil and, with the back of a wooden spoon, squash down on them lightly.

4 Roast for 30 minutes, turn the potatoes over and pop them back in for another 15–20 minutes till crispy. Season and serve.

✓ De-stress
Cook the potatoes a bit ahead of time and reheat until crispy and hot.

Sozzled Spanish Chicken & Almonds

The smoky boozy smell that fills the kitchen will have you salivating way before this hits the table. Try it served with Sweet Magic Kale (see p91) and Patatas Bravas (see p124) for a perfect Spanish supper.

For 4
Prep time... 5 mins
Cook time... 45 mins
❄

All you need is...

8 skin-on chicken thighs, leave bone in
1 tsp fennel seeds
1 tsp smoked paprika
1 tbsp olive oil
3 garlic cloves, peeled
    and thinly sliced
50g toasted flaked almonds
zest and juice of 1 orange
200ml dry sherry (Fino if possible)
handful of fresh flat-leaf parsley,
    chopped, to serve

All you do is...

1 Preheat the oven to 200°C (fan), 220°C, gas mark 7. Trim away the excess chicken skin. Cut 2 deep slashes down through the skin and down to the bone on each thigh. Place in a bowl and sprinkle over the fennel seeds, smoked paprika and seasoning. Rub well into the chicken.

2 In a large frying pan, heat the olive oil and cook the chicken, skin side first, for 5 minutes until really golden, then turn and cook for 2 minutes. Transfer to a large casserole dish.

3 In the same frying pan, turn the heat right down and add the garlic for 1 minute then the almonds and orange zest and cook for 2 minutes, stirring. Add the sherry and orange juice and bubble for 4–5 minutes to reduce and burn off the alcohol. Pour over the chicken, then pop a lid on and bake in the oven for 30 minutes.

To serve
Throw over a handful of chopped parsley.

✓ De-stress
Get the chicken marinating in advance.
✓ Impress
Serve wearing a Sombrero.

Aaron's Amazing Feta, Bacon & Courgette Pesto Pasta

Basically, I was cooking on TV with the fabulous high-energy chef Aaron Craze (who certainly lives up to his name), when he made this pasta for me to taste and I fell in love – with the pasta not the chef. I took him at his word when he said I could pass it on to you in my next book. It's now a family favourite, so this is from him to me to you with love.

For 6
Prep time... 15 mins
Cook time... 25 mins

All you need is...

4 large courgettes (500g)
12 rashers smoked streaky bacon
500g dried tagliatelli

Pesto
20g bunch of fresh mint, leaves only
75g walnuts
100g baby leaf spinach
2 garlic cloves, peeled
200g feta, crumbled
170ml olive oil

All you do is...

1 For the pesto, in a food processor whizz the mint leaves, walnuts, spinach and garlic till completely chopped into fine crumbs. Add half the feta and all the oil with some pepper and whizz again briefly.

2 To prepare the courgette ribbons, just run a potato peeler down the length of the courgette and keep going all the way round, stopping at the seeded middle (chuck that bit).

3 Dry-fry the bacon in a griddle or non-stick frying pan for 8–10 minutes until really crispy. Remove and set aside. Fry the courgette ribbons in batches in the bacon fat till they start to char, about 3–4 minutes.

4 Meanwhile, cook the pasta in a large pan of boiling salted water, following the pack instructions. Drain.

5 Put the pasta back into the pan and toss with the pesto and courgette ribbons. Then break over the large strips of crispy bacon and scatter the rest of the feta over the whole lot.

To serve
Tip into a big bowl, serve with a green salad and wait for some big smiles.

✓ De-stress
Make the pesto up to 3 days beforehand and store in the fridge.

Crispy Sesame Kale

For 4 (side)
Prep time... 5 mins
Cook time... 10 mins

Is it seaweed? Is it crisps? Is it out of a packet? Is it stuck in my teeth? These were just some of the questions fired at me when I first made Crispy Sesame Kale. It's now on the menu all year round with anything even vaguely Chinese. It's also the healthiest snack I have up my sleeve. I'm so Gwyneth Paltrow!

All you need is...

200g bag kale
2 tbsp olive oil
2 tbsp sesame seeds
½ tsp sea salt

All you do is...

1 Preheat the oven to 180°C (fan), 200°C, gas mark 6. Toss the kale in the rest of the ingredients and spread over a large roasting tray.

2 Bake for 10–12 minutes until the edges start to crisp up. Make loads!

Moroccan Za'alouk Fish Supper with Couscous

Moroccan flavours have warmth, colour, punch and a little mystery. This smooth North African sauce is one of my favourites, especially with lemony couscous and can be used with lamb, chicken or just mix it with chickpeas.

For 4
Prep time... 15 mins
Cook time... 1 hour

All you need is...

6 medium aubergines
4 tbsp olive oil
4 garlic cloves, peeled and crushed
2 tsp smoked paprika
1 tsp ground cumin
400g tin chopped tomatoes
1 tsp harissa paste
4 x 150–175g skinless, boneless white
    fish fillets, e.g. cod or haddock
2 tbsp chopped fresh mint leaves

Couscous
250g couscous
juice of 1 lemon
2 tbsp olive oil

All you do is...

1 Preheat the oven to 200°C (fan), 220°C, gas mark 7. Cut 4 of the aubergines in half lengthways. Put them on an oven tray and rub the cut sides with 2 tablespoons of olive oil and some seasoning. Cut the other 2 aubergines into big bite-sized pieces, toss in a tablespoon of olive oil and spread out on a separate oven tray. Pop both trays in the oven for 30–35 minutes till the flesh of the aubergine halves are soft and the smaller pieces are crisping up. Set aside to cool slightly.

2 In a tablespoon of olive oil in a large non-stick frying pan, cook the garlic, paprika and cumin for a minute then add the tinned tomatoes and harissa paste. Stir over the heat for another minute.

3 Now scrape the flesh out of the halved aubergines into the tomato sauce, season and stir to completely combine. Keep the aubergine pieces to one side.

4 Put the fish fillets in a large ovenproof dish and cover with the sauce. Pop back in the oven for 30 minutes till the sauce is bubbling and the fish cooked through.

5 For the couscous, in a large bowl, just pour 350ml boiling water over the couscous. Cover and leave for 5 minutes. Fluff with a fork, season and dress with the lemon juice and olive oil.

6 Serve the fish on top of the couscous, scatter over the chopped mint and the aubergine pieces.

✓ De-stress
Make the sauce well in advance and then just assemble and pop it in the oven.

✓ Impress
Add a handful of pomegranate seeds if you have them.

My Quick Posh Fish Dinner

This really does impress with its delicious citrus salty dressing on top of flakes of soft fish with garlicky bean mash – looks fancy pants but is easy peasy.

For 4
Prep time... 10 mins
Cook time... 10 mins

All you need is...

4 tbsp olive oil
3 garlic cloves, peeled and crushed
2 x 400g tins cannellini
    or flageolet beans
drained juice of 1 small lemon
4 x sea bass fillets

Dressing

390g tin artichoke hearts, drained
200g tin olives stuffed with
    anchovies, drained
2 tbsp olive oil
juice of 1 lemon
1 bunch fresh flat-leaf parsley,
    finely chopped

All you do is...

1 For the mash, heat 1 tablespoon of olive oil in a medium pan and fry the crushed garlic for 1 minute. Stir in the beans and gently warm through, mashing as you go until you have a rustic texture. Vigorously stir through 2 tablespoons of olive oil, the lemon juice to taste and seasoning. Set aside to keep warm.

2 For the dressing, finely chop the artichoke hearts and olives into a medium bowl. Dress with the olive oil and lemon juice. Stir through the parsley.

3 In a large non-stick frying pan, heat 1 tablespoon olive oil and fry the sea bass fillets, skin down first, till crispy, about 3 minutes, then flip them over and fry for another 1–2 minutes till cooked and the fish flakes easily.

To serve

Spoon some mash onto each plate, top with a fish fillet, skin side up, and sprinkle over a couple of spoonfuls of dressing.

✓ De-stress
Use any white skin-on fish fillets such as bream, tilapia, basa, whiting or haddock.
✓ Impress
Try slashing the skin with a sharp kitchen knife for that restaurant feel.

Purple-red Cabbage

For 4–6
Prep time... 5 mins
Cook time... 45 mins

Red cabbage boiled half to death to celebrate Xmas is why I spent many years avoiding it. Thankfully this easy oven-braised recipe has turned me back on to this often forgotten veg. It definitely deserves a place not only on the festive table, but as a side dish to add colour and purple pizzazz to all your roasts and grills. Stick some baked herby sausages on top for a great mid-weeker. P.S. … why is it called red not purple cabbage?

All you need is...

1 red cabbage
a pinch of ground cloves
¼ tsp mixed spice
¼ tsp coarsely ground black pepper
3 tbsp runny honey
2 tsp salt
1 tbsp sherry vinegar

All you do is...

1 Preheat the oven to 200°C (fan), 220°C, gas mark 7. Discard the outside leaves then very finely slice the cabbage with a sharp knife or mandolin.

2 Scatter the cabbage into an oven tray, add all the other ingredients and mix. Pour over 150ml water. Cover tightly with foil and bake for 45 minutes. Serve.

✓ Impress
Google the answer to above question re red not purple in case someone asks. Add a splash of sherry to the cooking liquid.

✓ De-stress
Reheats really well, so it makes a great prepare-ahead side dish.

Sticky Pork with Egg-fried Vermicelli Noodles

This is good. This is quick. This is cheap. And this is easy to make. It's never going to let you down and everyone of all ages will love it.

For 4–6
Prep time... 10 mins
Cook time... 15 mins

All you need is...

100g unrefined golden caster sugar
500g trimmed pork tenderloin
1 tsp Chinese 5-spice powder
2 garlic cloves, peeled and crushed
2 tbsp light soy sauce
1 tbsp toasted sesame oil

All you do is...

1 Spread the sugar over the base of a large lidded non-stick frying pan and place over a fairly high heat. Leave it to melt, shaking it a little and not stirring it for 2–3 minutes. Lower the heat.

2 Cut the loin in half, place in a bowl and rub the 5-spice all over. Put the meat into the pan to cook for 1–2 minutes on all sides. Lower the heat, add the garlic, soy sauce and sesame oil, cover and cook for 15 minutes, turning the loins every now and then.

3 Remove the loins onto a board, slice into thin medallions and put back into the pan with all the sticky juices to cook for another 5 minutes, turning them a few times to coat.

To serve
Layer the pork on top of the noodles and drizzle over the sauce.

Egg-fried Noodles

All you need is...

200g fine egg noodles
1 tbsp groundnut or olive oil
4 salad onions, finely chopped
150g frozen petit pois
2 eggs, beaten
1 tbsp light soy sauce
1 tbsp toasted sesame oil

All you do is...

1 Cook the noodles as per the pack instructions. Drain.

2 In a wok or large frying pan, heat the groundnut or olive oil then add the onions and petit pois and cook for 2–3 minutes. Add the eggs to 1 corner of the frying pan and cook for a couple of minutes, breaking them up as they cook.

3 Throw in the drained noodles for a few minutes to combine with the egg mix then toss in the soy sauce and sesame oil to flavour.

✓ Impress
Scatter over a handful of toasted sesame seeds.

No-cook 2-Minute Tomato Pasta Sauce

Here's a terrific no-cook no-time pasta sauce that gets me out of jail free when all seems lost. Pick any pasta from tortellini to spaghetti. I've chosen penne because the sauce gets trapped in the tubes then bursts in your mouth to give little surprise tomato explosions – a save-your-arse special.

For 4
Prep time... 5 mins
Cook time... 10 mins

All you need is...

400g penne pasta
3 salad onions, roughly chopped
1 garlic clove, peeled and crushed
400g tin chopped tomatoes
2 tbsp mascarpone
grated Parmesan, to serve

All you do is...

1 Cook the pasta as per the pack instructions in plenty of boiling salted water.

2 Meanwhile, make the sauce. In a food processor, whizz the salad onions, garlic and tinned tomatoes until smooth. Add the mascarpone for just a moment to combine.

3 Drain the pasta and toss with the sauce.

To serve
Serve immediately with the parmesan, garlic bread and salad.

✓ De-stress
The sauce can be made as a big batch and stored in the fridge; it also freezes really well.

✓ Impress
Throw on some chopped fresh tomatoes and basil, if you have some around ... or make it meaty with a bit of fried pancetta or bacon.

My Big Mac

For 4
Prep time... 10 mins
Cook time... 30 mins

This has got my children addicted to fresh mackerel. Clearly a minor miracle has occurred and it's now Sonny's favourite fish dish. Tick that parenting box. I think it's the crispy, citrus breadcrumbs with salty pancetta that makes even kids who run away from fish fingers have a go. At least I've ticked one box ... 999 to go.

All you need is...

8 fillets fresh mackerel
2 tbsp olive oil
1 onion, peeled and finely chopped
100g diced pancetta (or smoked bacon lardons)
150g crustless sliced white bread
10 sage leaves
zest of 1 lemon
2 garlic cloves, peeled and crushed

All you do is...

1 Preheat the oven 200°C (fan), 220°C, gas mark 7. Remove all the pin bones from the fish. Heat 1 tablespoon olive oil in a large non-stick frying pan and cook the onion and pancetta for 5 minutes.

2 Blitz the bread, sage, lemon zest and garlic in a food processor to a chunky crumb texture. Add the crumbs to the onion mix in the frying pan with the remaining oil and fry for another 5 minutes, stirring till lightly golden. Season.

3 Lay 4 mackerel fillets on a lightly greased baking tray or dish, skin side down. Spoon over half the breadcrumb mixture. Pop another fillet on top, skin side up, to make a sandwich and top with the rest of the crumbs.

4 Bake for 15–18 minutes until the fish is cooked through and the topping crunchy.

To serve
Serve with roast potatoes. It is also great with Sweet Magic Kale (see p91).

✓ Impress
Pick a good-looking oven dish to cook them in so you can take it straight to the table.
✓ De-stress
Make the stuffing and pin-bone the fish in advance, I use my eyebrow tweezers to yank out the bones. If short on time (and patience), use a large kitchen knife at an angle to cut out the middle bones and dark centre of each fish fillet. Be careful to cut only a very thin strip out and not damage the skin.

One-pot Spiced Chicken with Apricot Rice & Mint Raita

This will fill your home with comforting exotic smells and will fill you with the sense of warmth and wellbeing that only a great one-pot dish can do.

For 4
Prep time... 10 mins
Cook time... 55 mins

All you need is...

2 tsp garam masala
8 skinless, boneless chicken thighs, trimmed
1 large onion, peeled and thinly sliced
1 tbsp olive oil
2 garlic cloves, peeled and crushed
1 tsp ground cumin
1 tsp ground cinnamon
80g ready-to-eat dried apricots, roughly chopped
250g brown basmati rice, rinsed
250g pack ready-to-eat Puy lentils
750ml hot chicken stock
100g toasted flaked almonds, to serve

All you do is...

1 In a bowl, rub the garam masala all over the chicken thighs and set aside.

2 In a heavy-based pan, soften the onion in the oil for 5–10 minutes. Then add the garlic for 1 minute. Now throw in the cumin, cinnamon and apricots for another minute or so. Stir in the rice, lentils and stock.

3 Bring to the boil and pop the chicken pieces on top. Lower the heat to a gentle simmer, cover and cook for 40 minutes till the chicken is cooked through and the rice just soft.

To serve
Serve with the mint raita and a bowl of toasted flaked almonds to scatter over.

Mint Raita

All you need is...

½ cucumber
300g low-fat Greek yogurt
2 tbsp finely chopped fresh mint leaves

All you do is...

1 Deseed the cucumber by cutting it in half down the middle and running a teaspooon down the seeded centre. Finely chop the flesh and add to the yogurt and mint. Season.

✓ De-stress
Use scissors to snip in the dried apricots.

My Big Fat Greek Shepherd's Pie

Feta cheese popping through lemony mash over a hearty, rich meat sauce makes this absolutely delicious and great as a shared dinner or lunch.

For 4–6
Prep time... 20 mins
Cook time... 1 hour 15 mins
❄

All you need is...

1 red onion
a splash of olive oil
500g lean minced lamb
2 tsp dried oregano
3 garlic cloves, peeled and crushed
1 red pepper, deseeded and chopped
200ml red wine (change to stock if
    not using)
300ml beef stock
2 tbsp tomato purée
50g black pitted Greek olives
    (Kalamata)

Mash
800g potatoes, peeled and diced
2 tbsp olive oil
juice of 1 lemon
30g bunch of fresh mint,
    leaves chopped
120g feta

All you do is...

1 Preheat the oven to 180°C (fan), 200°C, gas mark 6.

2 Put the potatoes on to cook for the mash. Place them in a large pan of salted water, bring to the boil and simmer for 20 minutes.

2 Meanwhile, in a large non-stick frying pan, fry the onion in the olive oil for 5 minutes. Add the lamb mince, turning till it browns, for about 5 minutes.

3 Stir in the oregano, garlic and chopped pepper and cook for another 5 minutes. Now add the wine and let it bubble away for 5 minutes more over a high heat. Stir in the stock and tomato purée for another 5 minutes. Drop in the olives and scrape everything into a medium-sized oven dish, about 3 litres.

4 Drain the potatoes, mash and then stir through the olive oil, lemon juice and chopped mint. Crumble in chunks of feta and some seasoning and gently mix together.

5 Fork the mash roughly on top of the mince, place the dish on an oven tray and bake for 30–40 minutes, till golden and bubbling.

To serve
Serve with lots of green vegetables.

✓ De-stress
Make beforehand, then bake for an extra 15 minutes from the fridge. It's even better the next day.

Sweet Pesto-baked Squash

For 4
Prep time... 10 mins
Cook time... 50 mins

Vegetarian food is at its best when everyone wants to eat it. This sweet squash can be coupled with salads or fish, lamb or roast peppers. The pesto seems to draw in those veg-shy visitors who wouldn't normally eat anything that hasn't got a heartbeat.

All you need is...

- 2 butternut squashes (approx 1kg each), halved lengthways
- 1 tbsp olive oil
- 2 heaped tbsp fresh pesto
- 2 heaped tbsp mascarpone
- 2 tbsp grated Parmesan

All you do is...

1 Preheat the oven 180°C (fan), 200°C, gas mark 6.

2 Deseed the squash halves and cut the long narrow end off each half. Put the bowl-like ends into an oven tray. Peel the long ends, chop into small cubes and add to the tray. Drizzle the lot with the olive oil and bake for 45–50 minutes till cooked and tender.

3 In a bowl, mix the pesto and mascarpone together, season, then stir through the small cooked cubes of squash. Divide the mixture between the squash bowls (scatter any left around the tin) and load some Parmesan on top of each.

3 Put back into the oven for 10 minutes till the Parmesan is melted and golden.

✓ De-stress
Buy the pesto.
✓ Impress
Make the pesto (see p143).

Sweet & Sour Pork

For 4
Prep time... 10 mins
Cook time... 15 mins
❄

Seriously delicious, this tastes like a Chinese takeaway from the good old days. Back then, takeaways were for Saturday nights or birthdays and if you really want to go old-school, swap the pomegranate for pineapple chunks, pop on a nylon shirt and serve in a tinfoil tub with a fag in your mouth.

All you need is...

500g trimmed pork tenderloin
2 tbsp groundnut or olive oil
2 garlic cloves, peeled and crushed
1 tbsp fresh ginger, grated
2 tbsp sweet chilli sauce
4 tbsp tomato ketchup
250ml hot chicken stock
1 tbsp runny honey
1 tsp cornflour
100g pomegranate seeds

All you do is...

1 Cut the pork tenderloin into small bite-sized pieces, then in a large non-stick frying pan, heat the oil.

2 Throw in the pork and brown on all sides for 8–10 minutes. Then stir in the garlic and ginger for another 1–2 minutes.

3 Now add to the pan the sweet chilli sauce, ketchup, stock and honey. In a cup, mix the cornflour with 1 tablespoon of water and stir that in too.

4 Bubble for 3–4 minutes till the sauce thickens and the pork is completely cooked through.

5 Take off the heat, throw in the pomegranate seeds and serve.

To serve
Great with plain rice and Crispy Sesame Kale (see p144).

✓ De-stress
Don't worry about peeling the ginger as the skin will be left behind in the grater.

Lemon &
Basil Summer
Spaghetti

A simple fresh pasta dish that my family just adores on a hot summer's night. You could serve it as a starter, as a lunch or as a light citrus supper. A storecupboard special.

For 4
Prep time... 10 mins
Cook time... 10 mins

All you need is...

400g spaghetti
100g pine nuts
juice of 2 lemons
1 garlic clove, peeled and crushed
150ml olive oil
100g Parmesan, finely grated
30g fresh basil leaves, torn

All you do is...

1 Cook the spaghetti in a large pan of boiling salted water, as per the pack instructions. Gently toast the pine nuts in a frying pan for 3–4 minutes, stirring till golden (watch them).

2 In a jug, whisk together the lemon juice, garlic, oil, Parmesan and a really good grind of pepper.

3 When the pasta is al dente, drain and put back in the pan. Mix with the cheesy lemon dressing, torn basil leaves and toasted pine nuts.

To serve
Serve alongside crusty garlic bread and green salad.

✓ De-stress
Mix the dressing beforehand.

Soy Roast Colly

A super easy way to jazz up colly. Serve with noodles or rice dishes, fish or chicken. I have turned around my kids by cooking it this way. Next challenge: sprouts.

For 4 (side)
Prep time... 5 mins
Cook time... 25 mins

All you need is...

1 large cauliflower head
1 tbsp olive oil
1 tbsp light soy sauce

All you do is...

1 Preheat the oven to 200°C (fan), 220°C, gas mark 7.

2 Cut the cauliflower head into florets, put in a roasting tin and toss in the oil and soy then roast for 25 minutes. Stir once. Serve.

✓ Impress
Serve with a sprinkle of chilli flakes and keep an eye out for interesting varieties of cauliflower.

'If ants are such busy workers,
how come they find time to
go to all the picnics?'
Marie Dressler

great outdoors

Fruit bowl with lime & mint syrup

Fresh white slaw

BBQ or baked masala salmon

A smoky cheese & onion tart

Tomato & apple chunky chutney

Smoked mackerel & chive tart

Sushi salad

Sticky glazed ham

Portuguese piri-piri chicken

Coronation chicken with pomegranate
& mint

Piggies in the middle

The vicar's pulled pork

A great Greek barbie

Niçoise potato salad

Chicken & chorizo burgers in brioche

great
outdoors

Fruit Bowl with Lime & Mint Syrup

Nature's blinking marvellous, isn't it? It's given us this vibrant fruit with an in-built bowl that looks like it's from a dessert island, tastes of sunlight and doesn't need washing up. Now I just need a handbag tree …

For 4–6
Prep time… 15 mins
Cook time… 5 mins

All you need is…

5 limes
5 fresh mint sprigs and leaves,
    plus some small leaves to decorate
80g granulated sugar
1 medium watermelon, halved
    or ½ a big one
1 small pineapple, peeled, cored
    and diced
double shot vodka … (optional)

All you do is…

1 First, zest 2 of the limes and set aside. Squeeze the lime juice from all the limes and strip the leaves from the mint sprigs.

2 Place the sugar in a small pan with the bare mint stalks and all of the lime juice. Do not stir but shake the pan a little till the sugar dissolves, but do not boil. Remove, discard the stalks and stir in the lime zest. Set aside.

3 Cut the flesh out of the melon halves with a big spoon to create 2 bowls. Deseed the flesh and cut into big bite-sized chunks. Place the flesh in a large bowl with the pineapple pieces and pour over the syrup (and vodka if using).

4. Finely chop the mint leaves and add to the fruit. Tumble the whole mix together and then re-fill the melon bowls with the fruit. Decorate with the small mint leaves.

To serve
Serve with forks and straws.

✓ De-stress
Wrap the filled melons in cling film for a picnic centrepiece.

Fresh White Slaw

This is a mega-useful side dish full of fresh crisp flavours that can be knocked up in minutes to go with almost anything.

For 6
Prep time... 10 mins
Cook time... None

All you need is...

1 small white cabbage (350–400g), quartered and core removed
2 fennel, trimmed and halved
2 red-skinned apples, cored and chopped into matchsticks
4 spring onions, very finely sliced
30g bunch fresh coriander, leaves chopped
1 fresh red chilli, deseeded and finely chopped

Dressing
4 tbsp extra virgin olive oil
juice of 3 limes
2 tbsp light soy sauce

All you do is...

1 Finely slice the cabbage and fennel. Transfer to a large bowl and add the apples, spring onions, coriander and chilli. Toss together.
2 Make the dressing by whisking together the oil, lime juice and soy sauce in a small jug. Just before you are ready to serve, pour it over the slaw and mix well.

✓ De-stress
Prep ahead by slicing everything and keeping in a large food bag in the fridge for up to a day. Mix in the dressing at the last minute.

BBQ or Baked Masala Salmon

For 4
Prep time... 5 mins
Cook time... 15 mins

This is so good with Fresh White Slaw (see p177). It's creamy with a twang and takes no time at all to rustle up. Kids love it and although you don't have to use the skewers, it definitely adds the oooohhhhh factor.
I like oooohhhhh's.

All you need is...

4 tbsp Greek yogurt
1 heaped tbsp Tikka Masala paste
1 lemon
**4 x 180–200g thick salmon fillets,
    skinned**

Equipment
4 bamboo skewers

All you do is...

1 Fire up the barbie or preheat the oven to 200°C (fan), 220°C, gas mark 7. Soak the wooden skewers in water for a few minutes.

2 In a wide bowl, mix the yogurt with the Masala paste and zest the lemon into it. Put the salmon fillets into the sauce and completely cover.

3 Line an oven tray with baking paper and lay each yogurt-covered salmon fillet next to each other in a line. Push all 4 skewers gently through the fish fillets to create a sort of fish grid.

4 If cooking on the bbq, lay the whole fish grid onto the grill and cook for about 7 minutes on each side depending on how hot it is. Alternatively, bake in the oven for 15–18 minutes till nearly cooked through (the fish will continue to cook a little once resting).

5 Take the fish to the table on a plate with the skewers intact and gently slide off the salmon. Serve with the lemon, cut into wedges, on the side.

✓ De-stress
Marinate the salmon in the yogurt sauce overnight. Leftovers can be used flaked over salads, or in wraps or sandwiches.

✓ Impress
Serve with some mango chutney drizzled on top.

A Smoky Cheese & Onion Tart

For 4
Prep time... 10 mins
Cook time... 40 mins

Lunches, picnics, play dates, Saturday brunch, this tangy tart is a lifesaver. You can, of course, use any grated hard cheese, but it's the smoke that makes grown-ups rip the last piece out of their kids' hands. This is homemade pizza without the pressure.

All you need is...

- a splash of olive oil
- 1 onion, peeled and finely sliced
- 1 tbsp fresh thyme leaves, roughly chopped
- 180g smoked Cheddar, e.g. Applewood, grated
- 200ml half-fat crème fraîche
- 320g pack ready rolled shortcrust pastry (or make it, see p48)
- 10 cherry tomatoes, halved

All you do is...

1 Preheat the oven 180°C (fan), 200°C, gas mark 6.

2 Heat the olive oil in a frying pan and fry the sliced onion till soft and starting to go golden at the edges, about 10 minutes. Throw in the thyme leaves and transfer to a large bowl along with the grated cheese and crème fraîche. Add some black pepper and mix well.

3 Unroll the pastry onto a lined baking tray. Fold over the edges of the pastry,1cm in, all the way around to give the tart an edge. Use a fork to press it into place and mark the border.

4 Spread the cheesy mix over the base of the tart and scatter with the tomato halves. Bake for 30 minutes till golden and bubbling.

To serve
Allow to cool slightly and serve on a big wooden board with a crisp green salad.

✓ De-stress
Get the pastry out of the fridge 15 minutes before unrolling.
✓ Impress
Serve with apple cider over ice and apple juice for the kids.

Tomato & Apple Chunky Chutney

For 3–4 jars (650g)
Prep time... 15 mins
Cook time... 35 mins

This is super easy to make but its uses are endless. Let it light up a picnic or be the icing on your cheese board. It's a gift that will thrill or a thank you for having me. I pair it up with my Sticky Glazed Ham (see p188), but you can just slap it on a sandwich or brighten up your breakfast with it.

All you need is...

1 red onion, peeled
  and finely chopped
1 tbsp olive oil
4 eating apples, cored and peeled
2 tsp mixed spice
½ tsp dried chilli powder
1 tsp ground cumin
1 tsp salt
3 tbsp light brown sugar
2 tbsp sultanas
1 tbsp balsamic vinegar
1 bay leaf
400g tin chopped tomatoes

All you do is...

1 In a large pan, fry the red onion in the olive oil for 5 minutes till soft. Dice the apples into very small cubes and throw them into the pan with the mixed spice, chilli, cumin, salt and a grind of pepper. Cook for 10 minutes then add the rest of the ingredients and simmer, uncovered, until the apples are soft, about 20 minutes.

2 Cool completely then spoon into sterilised jars with a piece of baking paper and a tight-fitting lid.

✓ De-stress
The chutney lasts 2–3 weeks in the fridge once opened.
✓ Impress
Stick a ribbon and label on the jar – think farmer's market vibe ...

Smoked Mackerel & Chive Tart

For 4–6
Prep time... 15 mins
Cook time... 45 mins

I often suggest opting for the very useful shortcut of ready-rolled pastry, but with this savoury quiche it makes all the difference if you make your own. It's meant to look rustic, which lets you off the hook, frankly, if your pastry isn't perfect. Great served warm or at room temperature, take it on a picnic with some Fresh White Slaw (see p177) or a green salad and Speedy Horseradish Soda Bread (see p84).

All you need is...

320g pack ready-rolled shortcrust
    pastry (or make your own, see p48)
2 large eggs, beaten
180g smoked mackerel fillets
100ml milk
200ml half-fat crème fraîche
3 tsp creamed horseradish
25g bunch fresh chives, chopped

All you do is...

1 Preheat the oven to 200°C (fan), 220°C, gas mark 7.

2 Roll out the pastry and line a 22cm tart or cake tin. Roughly trim the edges. Prick the base with a fork. Blind bake (with baking beans or rice on top of baking paper) for 15 minutes. Remove the paper and beans and brush the base all over with a little of the beaten egg and bake for another 5 minutes. Set aside.

3 For the filling, take the skin off the mackerel, tear the flesh into small pieces and scatter over the pastry.

4 In a large jug, gently whisk the milk, eggs, crème fraîche, horseradish and the chives with a good grind of pepper and pour over the mackerel.

5 Bake for 25–30 minutes on a baking tray until the top is golden and set.

✓ De-stress
Make the pastry case beforehand. If making the whole tart ahead and keeping in the fridge, just warm through in the oven.

Sushi Salad

For 4
Prep time... 10 mins
Cook time... 15 mins

This is definitely a family favourite of ours. I think because of the soft rice and gentle flavours it's a salad that kids greedily gobble down. So easy to put together after a busy day, it's full of healthy fresh ingredients with a wasabi and soy kick-ass dressing. Lunches for the girls, picnics with friends or show off at the office with a Tupperware full in the staffroom.

All you need is...

200g basmati rice, rinsed
1 whole broccoli head, cut into florets
120g fresh young leaf spinach
2 x 120g hot smoked or honey roast
   ready-cooked salmon fillets
2 ripe avocados, flesh chopped

Dressing
2 tbsp light soy sauce
juice of 3 limes
1 tsp runny honey
1 tsp wasabi paste
5cm fresh ginger, peeled
   and finely grated

All you do is...

1 Cook the rice in a medium pan with enough water to cover up to the first joint on your thumb, about 2.5cm above the rice. Bring to the boil, pop a lid on and simmer for 10 minutes, till slightly overcooked and sticky. Leave to cool completely with the lid on.

2 Steam the broccoli florets for just 2 minutes. Drain and refresh under cold water. Chop the broccoli into small pieces.

3 Finely slice the spinach leaves and throw in a bowl with the broccoli and cooled rice. Whisk the dressing ingredients in a small jug and toss through the salad.

4 Discard the skin from the salmon then just break up the fillets with your fingers over the top of the salad, and finally scatter with the avocado.

Sticky Glazed Ham

For 6–8
Prep time... 10 minutes
Cook time... 1 hour 25 minutes
❄ (after poaching)

I started cooking ham after years of begrudgingly paying a small fortune for wafer-thin slices wrapped in plastic. A cooked ham, smoked or unsmoked, is great value for money and can feed a huge crowd on a picnic or at a party. Plus, Xmas just isn't the same without one.

All you need is...

1–1.5kg boneless smoked
    gammon joint, tied with string
2 bay leaves
5 peppercorns
1 onion, peeled and halved
200ml apple juice

For the glaze...
4 tbsp thick-cut marmalade
2 tbsp grainy mustard

All you do is...

1 If you can, soak the gammon overnight covered in a pot of cold water. This is not essential but it does draw out some of the saltiness. Drain.

2 Pop the gammon into a very large pan, add the bay leaves, peppercorns, onion halves and apple juice. Then pour in enough cold water to cover. Bring to the boil, reduce the heat to a simmer, cover and cook for about an hour (to work out the exact cooking time, calculate 30 minutes per 500g).

3 Preheat the oven to 220°C (fan), 240°C, gas mark 9. Mix the glaze ingredients together.

4 When the ham is ready, drain and remove the fat, string and skin. Pop the ham into a foil-lined roasting tray and smother it all over in the glaze. Roast for 25 minutes. Cool completely before carving.

To serve
Serve buffet-style, thinly sliced on a platter with breads, cheeses, salads, pickles, mustards and my Tomato & Apple Chunky Chutney (see p182).

✓ De-stress
Defo one to do beforehand as it will keep really well loosely covered in the fridge for 5–7 days.

✓ Impress
Glaze a whole pig's head once you've mastered this … joking!

Portuguese Piri-piri Chicken

For 4
Prep time... 10 mins
Cook time... 40 mins
❄

I first had this over 10 years ago, not in Portugal but on Bondi beach with fries and a beer and I've been trying to recreate that moment ever since. Well, this is pretty damn close to the piri-piri Aussie daydream I remember, minus the blondes in thongs. Cook it on the barbie, or if not in the oven, and serve with a side of roasted or barbecued peppers and Patatas Bravas (see p124).

All you need is...

8 chicken thighs, skins on,
    bones cut out
1 tsp smoked paprika
1 tsp ground ginger
1 tsp dried oregano
1 tsp mild chilli powder
1 tsp sea salt
zest of 1 lemon
2 heaped tbsp tomato purée
1 tbsp olive oil

All you do is...

1 Fire up the barbie or preheat the oven to 180°C (fan), 200°C, gas mark 6. Trim the excess skin off the chicken pieces, leaving a top layer intact.

2 In a large bowl, mix the smoked paprika, ginger, oregano, chilli powder, salt and lemon zest. Add a good grinding of pepper then mix in the tomato purée and olive oil to a thick paste. Throw in the chicken thighs and thoroughly coat, massaging the paste into every nook and cranny.

3 Place the thighs as flat as possible on the bbq for about 8–10 minutes each side till cooked through, or place in a non-stick roasting tin and cook in the oven for 40–45 minutes.

✓ De-stress
Even better if left covered in the fridge to marinate overnight.
✓ Impress
Slice up with mayo and salad in a tortilla wrap.

Coronation Chicken with Pomegranate & Mint

Perfect for pop-ins, picnics or parties, if making this for a bigger gang, double the sauce then use a couple of ready-roasted chickens and shred the meat.

For 4
Prep time... 15 mins
Cook time... 20 mins

All you need is...

4 skinless chicken breast fillets
5 peppercorns
2 bay leaves
2 heaped tbsp mayonnaise
2 heaped tbsp low-fat Greek yogurt
2 heaped tbsp mango chutney
2 tsp mild curry powder
15g bunch fresh mint, leaves chopped
100g pomegranate seeds
50g toasted flaked almonds

To serve
2 naan breads, warmed
2 heads little gem lettuce,
    leaves separated

All you do is...

1 Poach the chicken breasts in a large pan by covering with cold water and throwing in the peppercorns and bay leaves. Bring to a simmer then cover and cook for 20 minutes till cooked through. Drain and cool completely. Dice up the meat.

2 In a large bowl, mix the mayonnaise, yogurt, chutney, curry powder and mint with seasoning. Stir a third of the pomegranate seeds into the sauce, add the cooled chicken and toss. Scatter generously with the almonds and the remaining pomegranate seeds.

To serve
Scoop up those creamy summer flavours with naan bread and gem leaves.

✓ De-stress
Keeps well, chilled in a plastic container. Scatter the almonds and pomegranate seeds just before serving.

Piggies
in the
Middle

In our house the Xmas tradition of 'Pigs in Blankets' and 'Devils on Horseback' have always been on the front line of some serious arguments, mainly about how many to cook or who gets the first pig or last devil. It often ends in an overly aggressive round of charades where odd-looking relatives point at naughty body parts and then at their husband or wife. So I combined these two morsels of festive fun and serve them at every picnic, party or snacky tea that I can ... These are definitely not just for Xmas fights.

For 18, serves 4–6
Prep time... 10 mins
Cook time... 35 mins
❄

All you need is...

9 streaky smoked bacon rashers
18 cocktail sausages
18 pitted dates

All you do is...

1 Preheat the oven to 180°C (fan), 200°C, gas mark 6. Snip the bacon rashers in half.

2 With a sharp knife or scissors, cut a hole in the side of each little sausage. Shove in a date as neatly as you can and wrap it in half a rasher. Place in a non-stick roasting tin.

3 Bake for 30–35 minutes shaking the tin a couple of times, till cooked and starting to char a little. Leave to cool.

To serve
Perfect for a picnic, as party food or alongside your Sunday roast chicken.

✓ De-stress
Stuff and wrap the little piglets in advance and keep in the fridge.

The Vicar's Pulled Pork

For 4–6
Prep time... 10 mins
Cook time... 2 hours
❄

This is one of those recipes that makes fellas go all gooey and flirty, constantly referencing how they like their pork pulled, etc ... It will affect uncles, your father-in-law, the bloke next door and vicars in equal measures. Just accept it and enjoy the fact that this is a real tasty crowd pleaser with very little effort from you.

All you need is...

2 tsp ground cumin
2 tsp smoked paprika
2 tbsp tomato ketchup
1 tbsp runny honey
zest and juice of 1 large orange
1.5kg boneless pork shoulder
   (or 2 smaller joints)
1 large onion, peeled and finely sliced

All you do is...

1 Preheat the oven to 150°C (fan), 170°C, gas mark 3. Mix the cumin, smoked paprika, ketchup, honey and zest of the orange together in a bowl.

2 Cut the fat off the pork and rub all over with the paste. Pop onto a bed of the sliced onions in a deep ovenproof pan or casserole dish and pour over the orange juice and 100ml water. Bung a lid on and roast for at least 2 hours. Check it a couple of times, it may need some boiled water from the kettle as it cooks to prevent the onions burning.

3 When ready, remove the pork from the pan to a plate and cover with foil. Then heat the liquid on the hob till it reduces to a thicker saucy consistency.

4 Pull that pork with 2 forks into shreds of moist morsels. Pour over the sauce and mix in.

To serve
Pile into squidgy buns with my Fresh White Slaw (see p177).

✓ De-stress
If your timings go AWOL and the guests are stuck in traffic, just leave that pork to cook away for 3–4 hours ... the meat just gets better.

A Great Greek Barbie

For 4
Prep time... 15 mins
Cook time... 30 mins & resting time

You can, of course, rub the lamb and cover, leaving it to absorb all those spices overnight in the fridge, but it's not essential. These are simple flavours to remind you that you don't have to be on holiday to eat sunshine food. Bung a few red peppers and some crusty bread on the grill to go with it.

All you need is...

½ tsp ground cinnamon
2 tsp ground cumin
2 tsp dried oregano
3 tbsp olive oil
½ boneless leg of lamb, 800g–1kg, butterflied (ask your butcher)

Dressing
juice of 1 lemon
handful of fresh mint leaves, chopped handful of pomegranate seeds

All you do is...

1 Mix the cinnamon, cumin, oregano and olive oil together in a large dish. Add the lamb and rub the meat all over with the marinade. Fire up the barbie.

2 Throw on the lamb and grill for 15–20 minutes each side, with the bbq lid down (use a foil-covered brick or rock to keep it flat if you want).

3 Remove and rest on a board covered with foil for 15 minutes. Slice thickly, transfer to a serving dish then dress with the lemon juice and mint and scatter over a handful of pomegranate seeds.

✓ De-stress
Alternatively, cook the lamb in the oven for the same time preheated to 200°C (fan), 220°C, gas mark 7.

Greek Salad

All you need is...

4 ripe vine-tomatoes
1 cucumber
handful of pitted olives
200g feta cheese, crumbled
1 tbsp fresh oregano or lemon thyme leaves, chopped

Dressing
2 tbsp extra virgin olive oil
2 tsp sherry vinegar

All you do is...

1 Roughly chop the tomatoes and deseed the cucumber by cutting it in half lengthways and running a teaspoon down the middle to remove the seeds, and discard them. Place in a serving bowl and add the olives, feta and fresh oregano.

2 Drizzle the oil and vinegar over and season.

✓ Impress
Create a stripy cucumber effect by alternately peeling strips of the cucumber skin with a vegetable peeler before cutting. Fancy!

Niçoise
Potato Salad

For 6
Prep time... 15 mins
Cook time... 20 mins

This is a perfect picnic pleaser or lunch-box favourite. One of my kids picks out the olives but the other doesn't, so by the rules of this house if someone likes them they stay in. Make your own rules and it'll become a storecupboard staple.

All you need is...

750g baby new potatoes,
    halve any big ones
200g green beans,
    trimmed and halved
200g jar or tin line-caught tuna,
    drained
3 big tbsp garlic mayo
1 tbsp olive oil
juice of 2 lemons
200g tin green olives stuffed with
    anchovies, drained
400g tin cannellini beans, drained
2 large hard-boiled eggs,
    roughly chopped
15g fresh chives, finely chopped

All you do is...

1 Place the new potatoes in a large pan of salted cold water and bring to the boil. Cook until they are tender and slip easily off a fork, about 15–20 minutes. Drain. Meanwhile, in a small pan of boiling water, blanch the green beans for 1–2 minutes. Refresh under cold water and drain.

2 For the dressing; either in a food processor or using a hand blender, whizz the tuna, garlic mayo, olive oil and lemon juice. Season with lots of pepper and a little salt.

3 In a large bowl, toss the cooked potatoes, tuna dressing, olives, cannellini beans, green beans and chopped eggs.

To serve
Serve with the chives thrown over.

✓ De-stress
Cook the potatoes and make the dressing in advance.
✓ Impress
Instant garlic bread: serve with griddle-marked ciabatta halves drizzled with olive oil and rubbed with a cut garlic clove.

Chicken & Chorizo Burgers in Brioche

I love a burger. I love a burger with a twist. I love the sweet brioche bun with that salty chorizo. Think Saturday brunch or Friday play dates, lads' nights out or girls' nights in. They'll all love it.

For 4
Prep time... 10 mins (plus chilling)
Cook time... 20 mins
❆ (uncooked burgers)

All you need is...

200g soft cooking chorizo
300g chicken or turkey mince
1 tsp dried oregano
1 dsp olive oil (optional)

To serve
400g brioche loaf
200g jar oven-roasted peppers, drained
2 tomatoes, sliced

All you do is...

1 Remove the skin from the chorizo, chop roughly and put it in a food processor with the chicken mince, oregano and seasoning. Whizz till totally combined. With damp hands, divide into 4 flat patties around 9–10cm wide. Place on a plate, cover and pop in the fridge for at least 20 minutes.

2 Preheat the bbq to a medium-high setting; grill the patties for about 8–10 minutes on each side till cooked through. To fry, in a large non-stick frying pan, cook the patties in the olive oil for 8–10 minutes on each side till completely cooked through.

3 Cut 8 very thick slices of the brioche and if barbecuing pop them on the grill for just a minute each side to slightly char, or pop under the grill.

To serve
Assemble each burger using 2 slices of toasted brioche per burger to encase a layer each of peppers, tomato and chicken burger.

✓ De-stress
Make the burgers up to a day in advance. If you don't have a food processor, just combine with a fork and a bit of elbow grease.

✓ Impress
A good spoonful of garlic mayonnaise makes a delicious finishing touch.

'Seize the moment.
Remember all those women
on the *Titanic* who waved
off the dessert cart.'
Erma Bombeck

'After nines' salty chocolate mints

Bounty banoffee pie

Orange caramel sauce with salty pecan brittle

Ivy's apple & sultana dumplings

Chocolate cream cakes

Chuck-it-all-in chocolate tray bake

Lemon & pistachio cake

Showstopping hazelnut & raspberry pavlova

Strawberries & cream cakes

Quick lemon curd iced cream pots

Tea thyme shortbread

Silly ice cream sandwiches

My raspberry red yogurt cake

Rhubarb cake with cheat's orange custard

Galaxy Rice Krispies snaps with easy banana frozen yogurt

What a whizz sticky date pudding

Little chocolate & almond bombes

sweet stuff

'After Nines' Salty Chocolate Mints

For 40 sweets
Prep time... 15 mins (plus chilling)
Cook time... None

You can knock up these morsels of minty magnificence in minutes. Old-school creamy peppermint mouthfuls with a salty explosion that literally melt in your mouth, they will leave you with memories of the days when a grapefruit juice was an exotic starter, fondue would follow and the perfect 70s meal was finished off with a soft chocolate mint and an instant coffee.

All you need is...

500g icing sugar, sifted and 100g extra for dusting
1 tbsp condensed milk
2 tsp peppermint extract
100g dark chocolate
½ tsp sea salt flakes

All you do is...

1 In a large bowl, mix the sifted icing sugar and the condensed milk along with the peppermint extract and 2 tablespoons cold water. Bring it together with your hands, working it into a ball (add a little extra water if necessary but only in drops as you don't want it too wet).

2 Liberally dust some extra icing sugar onto a sheet of greaseproof paper and a rolling pin. Roll the icing to a rectangle about the thickness of a rich tea biscuit. With a sharp knife, cut as many bite-sized squares as you can. Dust each one with sugar and store on more greaseproof paper on a baking tray. Re-roll and cut out the leftovers.

3 Melt the chocolate in a glass bowl set over a pan of gently simmering water. Cool slightly. Then with a teaspoon, piping bag or food bag that has had a teeny hole cut into the corner, drizzle over the chocolate in a criss-cross pattern (let the designer in you free). Crush some salt flakes between your fingertips and sprinkle over the sweets immediately. Keep on the paper and pop in the fridge for a couple of hours.

✓ De-stress
Find the condensed milk that's sold in squeezy bottles to make life easier. These keep really well between greaseproof paper in a covered container in the fridge for up to a week.
✓ Impress
Look out for smoked sea salt – it's smokin'!

Bounty Banoffee Pie

For 8
Prep time... 15 mins (plus chilling)
Cook time... 5 mins

Let's face it it's not rocket science to put soft sticky bananas with a crisp coconut chocolate base and a creamy coconut topping. What is damn clever is making it when no one is coming over and there's only you at home to eat it. I'm smart, me.

All you need is...

100g butter, cubed
250g plain chocolate digestive
   biscuits
2 tbsp desiccated coconut
½ x 400g jar nutella chocolate spread
3 ripe bananas
200ml whipping cream
200ml coconut yogurt
a couple of squares of plain
   chocolate, for grating

All you do is...

1 Line the base of a 24cm springform cake tin.

2 Gently melt the butter in a pan. Crush the digestives in a food bag (double-bag it!) with a rolling pin, to fine crumbs.

3 Stir the crumbs into the melted butter along with the desiccated coconut and mix thoroughly. Scrape the crumbs into the cake tin and smooth the base down with the back of a dessertspoon till compact. Pop in the fridge for at least an hour or overnight.

4 Just before serving; spread the nutella over the base then slice over the bananas.

5 Whip the cream to stiff peaks. Gently fold in the yogurt and spoon over the top of the pie. Unmould the pie from the cake tin and gently transfer to a plate, discarding the lining paper. Grate over a little plain chocolate from your secret stash.

✓ De-stress
Make the base the day before if pushed for time.
✓ Impress
Decorate with chocolate curls; make big ones from melting a bar of chocolate and pour onto a tray. Let it set then scrape a big kitchen knife or hand-held cheese slicer along the surface. Alternatively, small ones are easy with a vegetable peeler and a bar of chocolate.

Orange Caramel Sauce with Salty Pecan Brittle

Warm or cold this is delicious, especially with the scattering of pecan crackle over the top. A bowl of fresh berries to go with it is a great option in the right season, but you'll find it hard not to snack on this salty, sweet brittle – so make plenty!

For 6
Prep time... 10 mins
Cook time... 20 mins

All you need is...

Nuts
3 tbsp golden caster sugar
1 tsp sea salt flakes
finely grated zest of 1 orange
100g pecan halves

Sauce
100g unsalted butter, cubed
60g golden syrup
60g golden caster sugar
1 orange
200ml double cream

To serve
vanilla ice cream
mixed berries

All you do is...

1 For the nuts, line a baking tray with baking paper. Scatter the sugar, salt and orange zest into a large non-stick frying pan. Put on a medium heat to melt. Don't stir but you can shake the pan to help it spread. Watch it while it melts. When melted and slightly caramelised, throw in the pecans and stir to coat. Immediately tip onto the lined tray and cool. When cold and hard, smash up or chop into smaller pieces.

2 For the sauce, just melt the butter, syrup and sugar in a small pan. Then add the zest of the orange and half of its juice. Let it bubble briefly then add the cream. Bring to the boil and simmer gently for 10 minutes to thicken. Pour it into a jug and cool. Keep in the fridge to thicken further.

To serve
Pour the sauce over vanilla ice cream.

✓ De-stress
Don't panic about washing up that sugary pan, just pour boiling water into it and leave to let the sugar dissolve. Can be made 2–3 days in advance. Keep the nuts in an airtight container and the sauce in the fridge.

Ivy's Apple & Sultana Dumplings

I remember as a child the excitement of arriving after a long journey dominated by car sickness and travel sweets at my Grandma Ivy's seaside bungalow. The sweet smell of fruit and pastry welcoming me into a world of pies, cakes and puddings, it is a world I have never quite left.

For 4
Prep time... 10 mins
Cook time... 35 mins

All you need is...

320g pack chilled ready rolled
   shortcrust pastry or Grandma's
   Perfect Pastry (p48)
2 tbsp light brown soft sugar
2 tsp mixed spice
4 small dessert apples, peeled
   and cored
4 tbsp sultanas
1 large egg, beaten
500ml custard or double cream,
   to serve

All you do is...

1 Preheat the oven to 180°C (fan), 200°C, gas mark 6. Line an oven tray.

2 Let the pastry come to room temperature for a while to soften. Unroll it and cut a thin strip off the short end, 2–3cm wide. From this, cut out 4 leaf shapes and draw veins with the end of a sharp knife. Cut the rest of the pastry into 4 squares.

3 In a small bowl, mix the sugar and spice. Roll each prepared apple in the sugar mix. Pop it in the middle of a square of pastry. Fill the hole with 1 tablespoon sultanas and fold up the sides of the pastry, gently pressing the pastry into place at the top. Use any excess to shape a little stork.

4 Pop a leaf shape on and gently pinch that into place. Brush the top half of the apple with the egg, cut a small slit in the top of the pastry and sprinkle all over with a little more of the spiced sugar. Repeat with all the apples.

5 Bake on the lined oven tray for 30–35 minutes till golden.

To serve
Place in a bowl and sit in a pool of custard or cream.

✓ De-stress
Prepare the wrapped apples up to 4 hours before and keep in the fridge till you are ready to cook. Cook for an extra 10 minutes.

✓ Impress
Put lots together on a large plate for greater effect.

Chocolate Cream Cakes

Makes 8
Prep time... 10 mins
Cook time... 25 mins (plus cooling)
❄

These cakes will delight all ages. They are rich, creamy and feel luxurious, so save them for dinners, puddings, special teas and late-night nibbles. They've taken over from the brownie in my house …

All you need is...

75g unsalted butter, cubed
100g dark chocolate, broken
    into pieces
150g full-fat cream cheese
    (Philadelphia)
100g unrefined golden caster sugar
1 large egg, beaten
50g ground almonds
50g plain flour, sifted
1 tsp baking powder, sifted
handful of pine nuts

Equipment
12-hole muffin tray and paper
    muffin cases

All you do is...

1 Preheat the oven to 180°C (fan), 200°C, gas mark 6. Line 8 holes in the muffin tin with paper muffin cases.

2 Melt the butter and chocolate together in a glass bowl set over a pan of simmering water. Make sure the bottom of the bowl doesn't touch the water. Cool slightly.

3 Using an electric whisk, mix the cream cheese and sugar for 1 minute then add the egg, ground almonds, flour and baking powder, mixing by hand. Pour in the melted butter and chocolate and fold together.

4 Spoon the mix into the muffin cases and sprinkle each with some pine nuts. Bake for 25 minutes. Cool briefly in the tin before removing.

To serve
Deliciousness itself served both warm or at room temperature.

✓ De-stress
These freeze really well so make a stack of them and warm through before serving.

✓ Impress
Remove the paper and serve warm in a pool of single cream for a grown-up pud.

Chuck-it-all-in Chocolate Tray Bake

For 16–20
Prep time... 20 mins
Cook time... 35 mins
❄ (cake freezable un-iced)

This solves more problems than I knew I had. It's a hand-me-down recipe from my brilliant baking sister, Elisa, who makes cakes, usually my recipes, for a living. I now make it for almost every birthday in some form or other. It's my staple for a school bake sale and is like the loaves and blinking fishes, as it can feed hundreds ... you just make the squares smaller and smaller, depending on your numbers. Thanks, sis. Now can you give me a cake recipe to pay my mortgage, walk the dog and stop my underarms hitting my face when I wave you goodbye?

All you need is...

40g cocoa powder
200g unsalted butter, softened
200g unrefined golden caster sugar
4 large eggs
250g self-raising flour
1 tsp baking powder
4 tbsp milk

Topping
140g apricot jam
120g dark chocolate
180g icing sugar, sifted

Equipment
30 x 20cm brownie tin or square
ceramic dish

All you do is...

1 Preheat the oven to 180°C (fan), 200°C, gas mark 6. Line the brownie tin with baking paper.

2 In a large bowl, first add the cocoa powder and 4 tablespoons hot water. Mix together, then add the butter and caster sugar and cream together with an electric whisk. Once smooth and fluffy, add the eggs, flour, baking powder and milk.

3 Whisk again until completely combined then scrape the mixture into your lined tin and bake for 35–40 minutes till firm to the touch. Cool completely before putting on a plate.

4 For the topping, spread the jam all over the top of the cooled cake with the back of a spoon. Now melt the chocolate in a glass bowl set over a pan of gently simmering water along with the icing sugar and 3 tablespoons water. Stir it all together then pour on top of the cake and smooth with the back of a spoon.

✓ De-stress
Make a day in advance but cut it up at the last minute.
✓ Impress
Decorate immediately with anything from sprinkles to chocolate curls (see p211).

Lemon & Pistachio Cake

Once this moist lemony marvel has christened your lips it will become your go-to cake for parties and puddings. Quite the best cake I make and now quite the best cake you make.

For 8
Prep time... 15 mins
Cook time... 45 mins
❄ (un-iced)

All you need is...

125g shelled pistachios
150g softened butter
150g unrefined golden caster sugar
150g self-raising flour
50g ground almonds
2 large eggs
juice of 2 lemons
½ x 300g jar lemon curd
75g icing sugar, sifted

All you do is...

1 Preheat the oven to 160°C (fan), 180°C, gas mark 4. Line the base of the 20cm springform cake tin with baking paper.

2 In a food processor, grind 100g of the pistachios (keep the rest for the top) to crumbs. Add the butter, sugar, flour and almonds and whizz to combine. Then pop in the eggs and whizz again. Finally, add the juice of 1 lemon and whizz to bring it all together.

3 Scrape half the mixture into the base of your tin and smooth it out. Then roughly spread the lemon curd over the top but not quite to the edge.

4 With the remainder of the mixture, drop dollops over the lemon curd layer to cover and gently smooth with the back of a spoon.

5 Roughly chop the rest of the pistachios by hand and scatter over the top. Bake for 45–50 minutes until golden brown. Cool completely in the tin.

6 For the icing, just mix together the icing sugar and 1½ tablespoons lemon juice, stirring into a paste. Criss-cross the top of your cake and leave for a couple of minutes to set.

✓ De-stress
This keeps really well covered for 2–3 days. If you don't have a food processor, use a coffee grinder for the pistachios and an electric whisk for the rest.

Showstopping Hazelnut & Raspberry Pavlova

For 8–10
Prep time... 15 mins
Cook time... 1 hour
❄ (Pavlova only)

I have had to include this showoff pud because although it's not a new idea it is one of the best party pieces I have up my sleeve. Make the meringues the day before, whip the cream a few hours in advance and keep it in the fridge. Then it's easy to assemble and even easier to eat. It can be a big birthday cake or a dinner party showstopper – you will be remembered for this one, trust me.

All you need is...

5 large egg whites
280g caster sugar
1 level tsp cornflour
1 tsp white vinegar
200g roasted chopped hazelnuts
   (buy the ready-to-go packs)
500ml whipping cream
400g raspberries
100g dark chocolate, broken
   into pieces

All you do is...

1 Preheat the oven to 130°C (fan), 150°C, gas mark 2 and line 2 baking sheets with baking paper.

2 With an electric whisk, whizz the egg whites until stiff, then whisk in the sugar, a dessertspoon at a time, until very thick and glossy.

3 Mix the cornflour and vinegar in a cup and whisk into the egg whites. Add most of the nuts, reserving a couple of tablespoons to decorate, and fold them in by hand (don't whisk at this point).

4 Divide the mixture between the 2 trays, gently spreading it into the shape you fancy (think about the plate it will sit on), keep the 2 shapes 2.5cm or so deep.

5 Pop the meringues into the oven and bake for 1 hour. Turn the oven off but leave them in there until completely cold or overnight – DON'T PEEK!

6 Before serving, whip the cream to soft peaks and then add half the raspberries. Carry on whipping and the cream will turn a gentle pink. Melt the chocolate in a glass bowl set over a pan of simmering water.

To serve
Use half the pink cream to sandwich the meringues together, using the rest on top. Scatter over the remaining raspberries, drizzle with the melted chocolate and finally scatter the remaining chopped nuts over your masterpiece. Take a bow!

✓ De-stress
You can use defrosted frozen raspberries for the cream.

Strawberries & Cream Cakes

Tea on a rolling lawn, Wimbledon, regattas … or sitting in the garden, these perfect English cakes will make you feel like you are to the Manor Born.

For 12
Prep time... 15 mins
Cook time... 20 mins
❄ (cake only)

All you need is...

200g butter, softened
200g caster sugar
2 large eggs
1 tsp vanilla extract
200g self-raising flour
3 tbsp milk
12 small strawberries, hulled

Topping
300ml whipping cream
2 tbsp icing sugar

Equipment
12-hole muffin tin and paper
   muffin cases

All you do is...

1 Preheat the oven to 180°C (fan), 200°C, gas mark 6. Line the muffin tin with paper muffin cases. Using an electric whisk, cream the butter and caster sugar together till fluffy. Add the eggs, one at a time, with the vanilla, beating in between. Fold in the flour and then the milk.

2 Divide among the cases and bake for 20 minutes till golden and firm. Cool for 2 minutes in the tin then remove to a wire rack to cool completely.

3 Carefully cut a 1p coin-size hole in the top of each cake with a small, sharp knife (the spare bits are the cook's perk). Now gently push a whole strawberry into each hole.

4 To make the topping, with an electric whisk, whip the cream and icing sugar until fairly stiff. Spoon the cream into a large food bag and snip a little hole in one corner. Pipe the cream topping in whirly round swirls onto the cakes.

✓ De-stress
Best on the day but not half bad the next day if kept in the fridge.

Quick Lemon Curd Iced Cream Pots

Oh God, these are good and, oh God, these are easy … need I say more?

For 6
Prep time... 5 mins (plus freezing)
Cook time... None
❄

All you need is...

300ml whipping cream
300g jar lemon curd

Equipment
6 ramekins or dessert dishes

All you do is...

1 Whip the cream till it forms soft peaks then add about ¾ of the jar of lemon curd. Whip again till combined and fluffy.

2 Spoon the lemon cream into 6 ramekins or dessert dishes, not quite to the top. Plop 1 teaspoon of extra lemon curd on top of each and freeze for ½–2 hours (it's best when still slightly soft).

To serve
Serve straight from the freezer with some Tea Thyme Shortbread fingers (p228).

✓ Impress
Make quick crystallised lemon to decorate by peeling off the zest from a lemon and snipping into thin strips. Add to a pan with 50ml water and 50ml caster sugar. Boil rapidly for 5 minutes, drain and cool in a sieve. Impress kids by scattering a chopped-up Crunchie bar on top.

Tea Thyme Shortbread

I make these a lot and they freeze brilliantly. You can swap the thyme for rosemary or lavender, but any which way they are totally delicious, crumbly and melt-in-the-mouth moreish.

For 16
Prep time... 10 mins
Cook time... 20 mins
❄

All you need is...

250g plain flour
a generous pinch of salt
80g caster sugar,
    plus extra for sprinkling
2 tbsp fresh thyme leaves
175g butter, softened
2 tsp caster sugar, for sprinkling

All you do is...

1 Preheat the oven to 180°C (fan), 200°C, gas mark 6. Line an oven tray with baking paper.

2 In a food processor, whizz the flour, salt, sugar and thyme leaves together until the thyme is finely chopped into the mix. Add the butter and process again until the mixture forms a dough.

3 Gather it up into a ball (I find it easier to work with half at a time). Roll it out between 2 sheets of baking paper until it's 1cm thick.

4 With a long knife cut it into rectangle fingers and space out on your lined tray. Keep gathering up the extra bits of dough and re-roll.

5 Bake for 20 minutes till lightly golden. Sprinkle some sugar on each biscuit as soon as they come out of the oven. Leave to cool completely.

✓ Impress
As a gift, wrap 6 fingers neatly in baking paper and tie with string.

Silly Ice cream Sandwiches

For 12
Prep time... 5 mins (plus freezing)
❄

This is more of a 'bloody' good idea than a 'bloody' good recipe ... you'll thank me for it though. You can use your favourite biscuits – try mini ones with different-flavoured ice creams. Just have fun. Serve the mini sandwiches with coffee after dinner or as a sweet canapé. Keep a tray full of them in the freezer for drop-ins from little kids looking for a treat and grown-up kids looking for ... well, a treat.

All you need is...

500ml tub best vanilla ice cream
2 x 12 packs Jaffa cakes

All you do is...

1 Using about 2 heaped teaspoons of softened ice cream, just sandwich together a couple of Jaffa cakes. Run a finger around the filling to smooth the sides.

2 Freeze immediately and leave to set for ½ hour at least.

✓ De-stress
Chocolate digestives work brilliantly.

My Raspberry Red Yogurt Cake

For 8
Prep time... 20 mins
Cook time... 50 mins
❄ (freezable but separately)

The dense texture of this cake with its bright fruit syrup makes this a fantastic pudding to show off with. It works brilliantly well baked in a Bundt cake mould, but is also lush in a round cake tin. Pile up high with the extra fruit, dollop on the cream and don't expect any leftovers.

All you need is...

150g unsalted butter, softened
250g caster sugar
2 large eggs
250ml natural yogurt
1 tsp vanilla extract
250g plain flour, sifted
2 tsp baking powder, sifted
225g raspberries, plus 225g extra
    to serve
80g icing sugar, sifted
juice of 1 lemon
whipped cream, to serve

Equipment
25cm Bundt mould or 20cm
    springform cake tin

All you do is...

1 Preheat the oven to 160°C (fan), 180°C, gas mark 4. Grease the Bundt mould (if using a tin, line the base with baking paper and lightly grease the base and sides).

2 Using an electric whisk, cream the butter and caster sugar together till fluffy. Add the eggs one at a time, beating well in between. Then whisk in the yogurt and vanilla (don't overdo it).

3 Fold in the flour and baking powder to combine. Plop it into your mould or tin, roughly smooth the top and bake for 50 minutes till golden and springy. Leave to cool slightly in the tin while you make the sauce.

4 In a blender, whizz up the raspberries, icing sugar and lemon juice. Pour the sauce through a sieve and discard the seeds.

5 If using a mould, pop a plate on top and flip the cake over then carefully ease the mould off. Or gently ease your cake out of the cake tin. Pour over the sauce while still warm.

To serve
Serve with the extra raspberries piled on top or in the hole and whipped cream on the side.

✓ De-stress
This cake is especially good served cold from the fridge.

Rhubarb Cake with Cheat's Orange Custard

You are either a hot custard person or a cold custard person. It's like being a scone or scowne … Tea with one or tea with none. Sex with costumes or sex without. Well, I'm in the cold custard gang, that's for sure. I feel less certain about the costume issue.

For 8 good slices
Prep time… 15 mins
Cook time… 40 mins

All you need is…

350g rhubarb, washed and trimmed
200g unrefined golden caster sugar
150g unsalted butter, softened
2 large eggs
zest and juice of 1 large orange
100g ground almonds
100g self-raising flour, sifted
1 tbsp demerara sugar
500g pot fresh ready-made
    custard, to serve

All you do is…

1 Preheat the oven to 180°C (fan), 200°C, gas mark 6. Line the base of a 22cm round cake tin and lightly grease.

2 Chop the rhubarb into 2cm bite-sized chunks, put in a bowl and toss in 50g of the caster sugar. Set aside.

3 In a large mixing bowl, cream the rest of the caster sugar and butter with an electric hand whisk until fluffy. Continue to whisk in one egg at a time followed by the orange zest. (Hang on to the juice.)

4 Fold in the almonds and flour and then the rhubarb. Scrape the thick mixture into the tin. Scatter the demerara sugar over the top, place on a baking tray and bake for 40 minutes till firm and golden. Cool completely in the tin.

5 Whisk the orange juice into the custard and keep in the fridge until you need it.

To serve
Serve with hot or cold custard depending on whose gang you are in.

✓ De-stress
Great made the day before, covered and kept in the fridge, but mix the custard on the day.

Galaxy Rice Krispies Snaps with Easy Banana Frozen Yogurt

Makes 16 squares
Prep time... 5 mins (plus chilling)
Cook time... 5 mins

Two great easy recipes to have together or by themselves …

All you need is...

200g Galaxy chocolate, broken into pieces
120g Rice Krispies

All you do is...

1 Line a 28 x 22cm brownie tin with baking paper.

2 Slowly melt the chocolate in a glass bowl set over a pan of gently simmering water. Take off the heat, add the Rice Krispies and carefully mix together.

3 Scrape into the brownie tin and gently smooth down the surface with the back of a large spoon so it fuses together and is completely flat. Pop in the fridge for 2 hours or overnight.

To serve
When completely cold and hard, ease out of the tin and cut with a large sharp knife into 16 squares of deliciousness.

Frozen yogurt PTO...

✓ Impress
If serving for a kid's party, decorate the top with mini marshmallows or small Smarties pressed into the top before setting.

Easy Banana
Frozen Yogurt

For 4
Prep time... 5 mins

All you need is...

4 large ripe bananas, peeled
200g (about 8 tbsp) Greek-style yogurt
1 big tbsp runny honey

All you do is...

1 Chop up the bananas and freeze in a food bag for at least an hour.

2 In a food processor, whizz the frozen banana pieces, yogurt and honey (think Mr Whippy in consistency).

To serve
Eat immediately!

✓ Impress
Serve with a scattering of berries.
✓ De-stress
Have the sliced-up bananas ready to go in the freezer for up to a month. Just take the bag out 15 minutes before making.

What a Whizz Sticky Date Pudding

This is ridiculously easy. You literally whizz it up in a food processor and as if by blinking magic it turns into everyone's favourite pudding. It's light but sweet and smooth with a caramel sauce that you'll lick off the plate. Feel free to lick the sauce off everyone else's plate too.

For 8
Prep time... 15 mins
Cook time... 30 mins
❄ (sponge only)

All you need is...

200g pitted dates
1 tsp bicarbonate soda
200ml boiled water
100g unsalted butter, softened
100g soft light brown sugar
150g self-raising flour
2 large eggs
vanilla ice cream, to serve

Sauce
150g soft brown sugar
150g butter
250ml single cream

All you do is...

1 Preheat the oven to 180°C (fan), 200°C, gas mark 6. Line and grease an ovenproof dish, about 22 x 22cm.

2 Put the dates, bicarbonate of soda and boiled water into a food processor. Remove the funnel from the lid so the steam can escape and whizz till smooth. Add all the other cake ingredients and whizz again till completely combined.

3 Scrape the mixture into your dish and bake for 30 minutes. Cool for 5 minutes.

4 Meanwhile, make the sauce by melting the sugar and butter completely. Take off the heat and stir in the cream. Put back on the heat and bubble for a few minutes to thicken slightly.

To serve
Just slice the cake into square portions and pour the hot sauce over each piece. Top with a scoop of vanilla ice cream.

✓ De-stress
You can make both the cake and sauce beforehand then gently reheat, but this one is so easy that you might not need to.
✓ Impress
Serve neat round puddings using a sharp circular biscuit cutter.

Little Chocolate & Almond Bombes

Simple, soft and moreish macaroon mouthfuls, these are perfect for afternoons and after dinner, or pop them into picnic baskets and lunch boxes as a surprise.

Makes 28–30
Prep time... 15 mins
Cook time... 15 mins

All you need is...

100g dark chocolate,
   broken into pieces
200g ground almonds
120g caster sugar
1 heaped tbsp cocoa powder
3 large egg whites
icing sugar, for dusting

All you do is...

1 Preheat the oven to 180°C (fan), 200°C, gas mark 6. Line a couple of baking trays with baking paper.

2 Melt the chocolate in a glass bowl set over a pan of simmering water. Cool.

3 Mix the ground almonds, sugar and cocoa in a large bowl. In another bowl (preferably metal or glass), whisk the egg whites until soft peaks then gently add to the chocolate mix and fold the 2 mixtures together.

4 With damp hands, roll a conker-sized ball of the dough and pop each one on the lined tray. Bake for 15 minutes, cool for 5–10 minutes before easing off the paper and dusting with icing sugar.

✓ De-stress
These will keep for 2–3 days in an airtight container.

Fay's Favourite Combos: Menu ideas to mix & match

Sunday Special...

Smoked salmon brioche mouthfulls (p103)

Royal Brittania roast lamb with a herby bean dressing (p80)

Rough rustic roasties (p139)

Purple-red Cabbage (p151)

Ivy's apple and sultana dumplings (p215)

Fresh & Light...

Parma ham and melon risotto (p56)

My seaside quick roast (p69)

A green salad

Crusty bread

Quick lemon curd iced cream pots (p226) with Tea thyme shortbread (p228)

Show-off to the Boss...

Scandi sharing plate (p112)

My quick posh fish dinner (p148)

Showstopping hazelnut & raspberry pavlova (p223)

Greek Holiday...

Taramasalata with baby tomato salad (p55)

A great Greek Barbie (p199)

Nutty green roast veg gratin (p64)

Garlic bread

Silly ice cream sandwiches (p231)

Let the Sun Shine...

Sweet fresh duck salad (p79)

Baked tahini salmon (p87)

Speedy horseradish soda bread (p84)

Roasted asparagus

Lemon & pistachio cake (p220)

Far East Feast...

San choy bau (p111)

Sweet miso fish with creamy coconut rice (p130)

Crispy sesame kale (p144)

Bounty banoffee pie (p211)

A Summer Table...

Antipasti sharing plate (p107)

Lemon & basil summer spaghetti (p166)

A green salad

Fruit bowl with lime and mint syrup (p174)

Comfort Eating...

Roasted tomato & pepper soup with sweet basil yoghurt (p59)

Poached Chinese chook (p67)

Minted peas

What a whizz sticky date pudding p241)

Chinese Take-away...

Sesame prawn toasts (p104)

Sweet & sour pork (p165)

'After nine' salty chocolate mints (p208)

Fortune cookies

Meat-free Feast...

Sweetcorn & mint fritters with griddles halloumi (p88)

Lentil-stuffed peppers with falafel topping (p63)

Whole roast colly with a lemon Parmesan dressing (p76)

Sweet pesto-baked squash (p162)

My raspberry yoghurt cake (p232)

Picnic Party...

Niçoise potato salad (p200)

Smoked mackerel & chive tart (p185)

Fresh white slaw (p177)

A big slab of cheese

Tomato & apple chutney (p182)

Chocolate cream cakes (p216)

La Fiesta!...

Parce the Spanish parcels (p108)

Sozzled Spanish chicken & almonds (p140)

Patatas Bravas (p124)

Sweet magic kale (p91)

Little chocolate & almond bombes (p242)

Index

Thank yous

It takes more than just me pootling about in my kitchen to make a book like this …

Parker, Sonny and Dan … aren't we something?
Paul … you still take my calls. Result
Anna … hopefully my best yet. Thank you
Maja and Simon … your pics will make them dribble
Bren … I only write books so I can still call you
Annie … you cook my recipes as if I've known you since junior school
Elisa … you wash up and prep with style and sweetness
George … with thanks for your hard work
Lucy and Martin … it's the prettiest one so far
Lydia and Olivia … God, I love your stuff
Laura and Virginia … thanks for schlepping me all over town
Julie … it's down to you now
Zoe and Charlotte … thanks for making sure I didn't look like a bloke in a dress
Carole … thanks for having me back
Tefal … your pots and pans make me a better cook, frankly
betsysbake.co.uk … your cakes inspire me
Halo Cooltouch … I'm even barbecuing for breakfast now

To you all, thank you from the bottom of my biscuit barrel

Fay x

HarperCollins*Publishers*
77–85 Fulham Palace Road,
Hammersmith, London W6 8JB

www.harpercollins.co.uk

First published by HarperCollins*Publishers* 2014

10 9 8 7 6 5 4 3 2 1

Text © Fay Ripley 2014
Photography © Maya Smend 2014

Fay Ripley asserts the moral right to be identified as the author of this work

A catalogue record of this book is available from the British Library

ISBN 978-0-00-754316-8

Food stylist: Annie Hudson
Props stylists: Lydia Brun and Olivia Wardle

Printed and bound in China by South China Printing Co. Ltd.